PRAXIS
PRINCIPLES OF LEARNING AND TEACHING (K-6) 5622

By: Sharon Wynne, M.S.

XAMonline, INC.
Boston

Library of Congress Cataloging-in-Publication Data

Wynne, Sharon A.
    PRAXIS Principles of Learning and Teaching (K-6) 5622 / Sharon A. Wynne.
    ISBN 978-1-60787-494-2
    1. Principles of Learning and Teaching (K-6) 5622
    2. Study Guides
    3. PRAXIS
    4. Teachers' Certification & Licensure
    5. Careers

Disclaimer:
The opinions expressed in this publication are the sole works of XAMonline and were created independently from the National Education Association, Educational Testing Service, or any State Department of Education, National Evaluation Systems or other testing affiliates.

Between the time of publication and printing, state specific standards as well as testing formats and Web site information may change and therefore would not be included in part or in whole within this product. Sample test questions are developed by XAMonline and reflect content similar to that on real tests; however, they are not former test questions. XAMonline assembles content that aligns with state standards but makes no claims nor guarantees teacher candidates a passing score. Numerical scores are determined by testing companies such as NES or ETS and then are compared with individual state standards. A passing score varies from state to state.

Printed in the United States of America   œ-1

PRAXIS Principles of Learning and Teaching (K-6) 5622
ISBN: 978-1-60787-494-2

Table of Contents

DOMAIN II

DOMAIN IV
PROFESSIONAL DEVELOPMENT, LEADERSHIP, AND COMMMUNITY 123

SAMPLE TEST 141

Three Full Practice Tests

NOW WITH ADAPTIVE ASSESSMENTS!

Adaptive learning is an educational method which uses computers as interactive teaching devices. Computers adapt the presentation of educational material according to students' learning needs, as indicated by their responses to questions. The technology encompasses aspects derived from various fields of study including computer science, education, and psychology.

In Computer Adaptive Testing (CAT), the test subject is presented with questions that are selected based on their level of difficulty in relation to the presumed skill level of the subject. As the test proceeds, the computer adjusts the subject's score based on their answers, continuously fine-tuning the score by selecting questions from a narrower range of difficulty.

The results are available immediately, the amount of time students spend taking tests decreases, and the tests provided more reliable information about what students know—especially those at the very low and high ends of the spectrum. With Adaptive Assessments, the skills that need more study are immediately pinpointed and reported to the student.

Adaptive assessments provide a unique way to assess your preparation for high stakes exams. The questions are asked at the mid-level of difficulty and then, based on the response, the level of difficulty is either increased or decreased. Thus, the test adapts to the competency level of the learner. This is proven method which is also used by examinations such as SAT and GRE. The Adaptive Assessment Engine used for your online self-assessment is based on a robust adaptive assessment algorithm and has been validated by a large pool of test takers. Use this robust and precise assessment to prepare for your exams.

Our Adaptive Assessments can be accessed here:

http://xamonline.4dlspace.com/AMOL/index.php?page=register

You will be presented with a short form
to complete for your account registration.
You will need an active email address to register.

Interactive Test

This test includes content from all three practice tests. It can be gone through sequentially by skill, or laterally. It can also be gone through horizontally, by skipping to a particular skill. The Question Difficulty Level goes up and down depending on your answers. All three Question Difficulty Levels—EASY, AVERAGE, and RIGOROUS—are included in this test. Feedback is given after every question. Questions are scored and reported every ten questions and at the end of the test. Reports are given by question and by Skill.

Level 1 Test

This test is comprised of Easy and Average test questions only. The Question Difficulty Level goes up and down between Easy and Average, depending on your answers. It moves sequentially by skill. This test includes content from all three practice tests. Feedback is given after every question. Questions are scored and reported every ten questions and at the end of the test. Reports are given by question and by Skill.

Level 2 Test

This test is comprised of Average and Rigorous test questions only. The Question Difficulty Level goes up and down between Average and Rigorous, depending on your answers. It moves sequentially by skill. This test includes content from all three practice tests. Feedback is given after every question. Questions are scored and reported every ten questions and at the end of the test. Reports are given by question and by Skill.

Practice Test

This test is comprised of questions from all tests and is timed and weighted to the actual test at 20/60/20. It includes time on question as well as time on test. All three Question Difficulty Levels are included in this test; the Question Difficulty Level goes up or down depending on your answers. Questions are scored and reported every 10 questions and at the end of the test. Reports are given by question and by Skill.

PRAXIS

PRINCIPLES OF LEARNING AND TEACHING (K-6) 5622

SECTION 1
ABOUT XAMONLINE

XAMonline—A Specialty Teacher Certification Company

Created in 1996, XAMonline was the first company to publish study guides for state-specific teacher certification examinations. Founder Sharon Wynne found it frustrating that materials were not available for teacher certification preparation and decided to create the first single, state-specific guide. XAMonline has grown into a company of over 1,800 contributors and writers and offers over 300 titles for the entire PRAXIS series and every state examination. No matter what state you plan on teaching in, XAMonline has a unique teacher certification study guide just for you.

XAMonline—Value and Innovation

We are committed to providing value and innovation. Our print-on-demand technology allows us to be the first in the market to reflect changes in test standards and user feedback as they occur. Our guides are written by experienced teachers who are experts in their fields. And our content reflects the highest standards of quality. Comprehensive practice tests with varied levels of rigor means that your study experience will closely match the actual in-test experience.

To date, XAMonline has helped nearly 600,000 teachers pass their certification or licensing exams. Our commitment to preparation exceeds simply providing the proper material for study—it extends to helping teachers **gain mastery** of the subject matter, giving them the **tools** to become the most effective classroom leaders possible, and ushering today's students toward a **successful future**.

SECTION 2
ABOUT THIS STUDY GUIDE

Purpose of This Guide

Is there a little voice inside of you saying, "Am I ready?" Our goal is to replace that little voice and remove all doubt with a new voice that says, "I AM READY. **Bring it on!**" by offering the highest quality of teacher certification study guides.

Organization of Content

You will see that while every test may start with overlapping general topics, each is very unique in the skills they wish to test. Only XAMonline presents custom content that analyzes deeper than a title, a subarea, or an objective. Only XAMonline presents content and sample test assessments along with **focus statements**, the deepest-level rationale and interpretation of the skills that are unique to the exam.

Title and field number of test

→Each exam has its own name and number. XAMonline's guides are written to give you the content you need to know for the specific exam you are taking. You can be confident when you buy our guide that it contains the information you need to study for the specific test you are taking.

Subareas

→These are the major content categories found on the exam. XAMonline's guides are written to cover all of the subareas found in the test frameworks developed for the exam.

Objectives

→These are standards that are unique to the exam and represent the main subcategories of the subareas/content categories. XAMonline's guides are written to address every specific objective required to pass the exam.

Focus statements

→These are examples and interpretations of the objectives. You find them in parenthesis directly following the objective. They provide detailed examples of the range, type, and level of content that appear on the test questions. **Only XAMonline's guides drill down to this level.**

How Do We Compare with Our Competitors?

XAMonline—drills down to the focus statement level.
CliffsNotes and REA—organized at the objective level
Kaplan—provides only links to content
MoMedia—content not specific to the state test

Each subarea is divided into manageable sections that cover the specific skill areas. Explanations are easy to understand and thorough. You'll find that every test answer contains a rationale so if you need a refresher or further review after taking the test, you'll know exactly to which section you must return.

How to Use This Book

Our informal polls show that most people begin studying up to eight weeks prior to the test date, so start early. Then ask yourself some questions: How much do you really know? Are you coming to the test straight from your teacher-education program or are you having to review subjects you haven't considered in ten years? Either way, take a **diagnostic or assessment test** first. Also, spend time on sample tests so that you become accustomed to the way the actual test will appear.

This guide comes with an online diagnostic test of 30 questions found online at *www.XAMonline.com*. It is a little boot camp to get you up for the task and reveal things about your compendium of knowledge in general. Although this guide is structured to follow the order of the test, you are not required to study in that order. By finding a time-management and study plan that fits your life you will be more effective. The results of your diagnostic or self-assessment test can be a guide for how to manage your time and point you toward an area that needs more attention.

After taking the diagnostic exam, fill out the **Personalized Study Plan** page at the beginning of each chapter. Review the competencies and skills covered in that chapter and check the boxes that apply to your study needs. If there are sections you already know you can skip, check the "skip it" box. Taking this step will give you a study plan for each chapter.

Week	Activity
8 weeks prior to test	Take a diagnostic test found at www.XAMonline.com
7 weeks prior to test	Build your Personalized Study Plan for each chapter. Check the "skip it" box for sections you feel you are already strong in. ✗ **SKIP IT** ☐
6-3 weeks prior to test	For each of these four weeks, choose a content area to study. You don't have to go in the order of the book. It may be that you start with the content that needs the most review. Alternately, you may want to ease yourself into plan by starting with the most familiar material.
2 weeks prior to test	Take the sample test, score it, and create a review plan for the final week before the test.
1 week prior to test	Following your plan (which will likely be aligned with the areas that need the most review) go back and study the sections that align with the questions you may have gotten wrong. Then go back and study the sections related to the questions you answered correctly. If need be, create flashcards and drill yourself on any area that you makes you anxious.

SECTION 3
ABOUT THE PRAXIS EXAMS

What Is PRAXIS?

PRAXIS II tests measure the knowledge of specific content areas in K-12 education. The test is a way of ensuring that educators are prepared to not only teach in a particular subject area, but also have the necessary teaching skills to be effective. The Educational Testing Service administers the test in most states and has worked with the states to develop the material so that it is appropriate for state standards.

PRAXIS Points

1. The PRAXIS Series comprises more than 140 different tests in over seventy different subject areas.

2. Over 90% of the PRAXIS tests measure subject area knowledge.

3. The purpose of the test is to measure whether the teacher candidate possesses a sufficient level of knowledge and skills to perform job duties effectively and responsibly.

4. Your state sets the acceptable passing score.

5. Any candidate, whether from a traditional teaching-preparation path or an alternative route, can seek to enter the teaching profession by taking a PRAXIS test.

6. PRAXIS tests are updated regularly to ensure current content.

Often **your own state's requirements** determine whether or not you should take any particular test. The most reliable source of information regarding this is either your state's Department of Education or the Educational Testing Service. Either resource should also have a complete list of testing centers and dates. Test dates vary by subject area and not all test dates necessarily include your particular test, so be sure to check carefully.

If you are in a teacher-education program, check with the Education Department or the Certification Officer for specific information for testing and testing timelines. The Certification Office should have most of the information you need.

If you choose an alternative route to certification you can either rely on our Web site at *www.XAMonline.com* or on the resources provided by an alternative certification program. Many states now have specific agencies devoted to alternative certification and there are some national organizations as well:

National Center for Education Information
http://www.ncei.com/Alt-Teacher-Cert.htm

National Associate for Alternative Certification
http://www.alt-teachercert.org/index.asp

Interpreting Test Results

Contrary to what you may have heard, the results of a PRAXIS test are not based on time. More accurately, you will be scored on the raw number of points you earn in relation to the raw number of points available. Each question is worth one raw point. It is likely to your benefit to complete as many questions in the time allotted, but it will not necessarily work to your advantage if you hurry through the test.

Follow the guidelines provided by ETS for interpreting your score. The web site offers a sample test score sheet and clearly explains how the scores are scaled and what to expect if you have an essay portion on your test.

Scores are usually available by phone within a month of the test date and scores will be sent to your chosen institution(s) within six weeks. Additionally, ETS now makes online, downloadable reports available for one calendar year from the reporting date.

It is **critical** that you be aware of your own state's passing score. Your raw score may qualify you to teach in some states, but not all. ETS administers the test and assigns a score, but the states make their own interpretations and, in some cases, consider combined scores if you are testing in more than one area.

What's on the Test?

PRAXIS tests vary from subject to subject and sometimes even within subject area. For PRAXIS Principles of Learning and Teaching (0622), the test lasts for 2 hours and consists of approximately 70 multiple-choice questions and 4 constructed response questions. The 70 multiple-choice questions are presented in four separate sections broken down as follows: 21 questions, 21 questions, 14 questions, and 14 questions each. The breakdown of the questions is as follows:

Category	Question Format	Approximate Percentage of the Test	Suggested Time to Spend on this Section
I: Students as Learners	Multiple-choice	22.5%	21 minutes

Table continued on next page

Category	Question Format	Approximate Percentage of the Test	Suggested Time to Spend on this Section
II: Instructional Process	Multiple-choice	22.5%	21 minutes
III: Assessment	Multiple-choice	15%	14 minutes
IV: Professional Development, Leadership, and Community	Multiple-choice	15%	14 minutes
V: Analysis of Instructional Scenarios A. Students as Learners B. Instructional Process C. Assessment D. Professional Development, Leadership, and Community	Constructed response	5%	50 minutes

Question Types

You're probably thinking, enough already, I want to study! Indulge us a little longer while we explain that there is actually more than one type of multiple-choice question. You can thank us later after you realize how well prepared you are for your exam.

1. Complete the Statement. The name says it all. In this question type you'll be asked to choose the correct completion of a given statement. For example:

> The Dolch Basic Sight Words consist of a relatively short list of words that children should be able to:
>
> A. Sound out
>
> B. Know the meaning of
>
> C. Recognize on sight
>
> D. Use in a sentence

The correct answer is C. In order to check your answer, test out the statement by adding the choices to the end of it.

2. **Which of the Following.** One way to test your answer choice for this type of question is to replace the phrase "which of the following" with your selection. Use this example:

> **Which of the following words is one of the twelve most frequently used in children's reading texts:**
>
> A. There
>
> B. This
>
> C. The
>
> D. An

Don't look! Test your answer. _____ is one of the twelve most frequently used in children's reading texts. Did you guess C? Then you guessed correctly.

3. **Roman Numeral Choices.** This question type is used when there is more than one possible correct answer. For example:

> **Which of the following two arguments accurately supports the use of cooperative learning as an effective method of instruction?**
> I.   Cooperative learning groups facilitate healthy competition between individuals in the group.
> II. Cooperative learning groups allow academic achievers to carry or cover for academic underachievers.
> III. Cooperative learning groups make each student in the group accountable for the success of the group.
> IV. Cooperative learning groups make it possible for students to reward other group members for achieving.
>
> A. I and II
>
> B. II and III
>
> C. I and III
>
> D. III and IV

Notice that the question states there are **two** possible answers. It's best to read all the possibilities first before looking at the answer choices. In this case, the correct answer is D.

4. **Negative Questions.** This type of question contains words such as "not," "least," and "except." Each correct answer will be the statement that does **not** fit the situation described in the question. Such as:

> **Multicultural education is not**
>
> A. An idea or concept
>
> B. A "tack-on" to the school curriculum
>
> C. An educational reform movement
>
> D. A process

Think to yourself that the statement could be anything but the correct answer. This question form is more open to interpretation than other types, so read carefully and don't forget that you're answering a negative statement.

5. **Questions that Include Graphs, Tables, or Reading Passages.** As always, read the question carefully. It likely asks for a very specific answer and not a broad interpretation of the visual. Here is a simple (though not statistically accurate) example of a graph question:

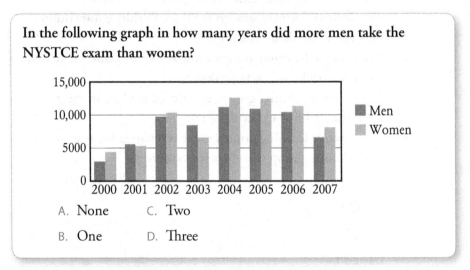

> **In the following graph in how many years did more men take the NYSTCE exam than women?**
>
> A. None C. Two
>
> B. One D. Three

It may help you to simply circle the two years that answer the question. Make sure you've read the question thoroughly and once you've made your determination, double check your work. The correct answer is C.

6. **Constructed response questions.** There will be 4 case studies and 4 constructed response questions. Constructed response questions require you to demonstrate your knowledge in a subject area by providing in-depth explanations on a particular topic. Essay and problem-solving are types of constructed response questions. A case history and supporting documents will be given to you in order to help you answer the question(s).

SECTION 4
HELPFUL HINTS

Study Tips

1. You are what you eat. Certain foods aid the learning process by releasing natural memory enhancers called CCKs (cholecystokinin) composed of tryptophan, choline, and phenylalanine. All of these chemicals enhance the neurotransmitters associated with memory and certain foods release memory enhancing chemicals. A light meal or snacks of one of the following foods fall into this category:

   - Milk
   - Rice
   - Eggs
   - Fish
   - Nuts and seeds
   - Oats
   - Turkey

   The better the connections, the more you comprehend!

2. See the forest for the trees. In other words, get the concept before you look at the details. One way to do this is to take notes as you read, paraphrasing or summarizing in your own words. Putting the concept in terms that are comfortable and familiar may increase retention.

3. Question authority. Ask why, why, why? Pull apart written material paragraph by paragraph and don't forget the captions under the illustrations. For example, if a heading reads *Stream Erosion* put it in the form of a question (Why do streams erode? What is stream erosion?) then find the answer within the material. If you train your mind to think in this manner you will learn more and prepare yourself for answering test questions.

4. Play mind games. Using your brain for reading or puzzles keeps it flexible. Even with a limited amount of time your brain can take in data (much like a computer) and store it for later use. In ten minutes you can: read two paragraphs (at least), quiz yourself with flash cards, or review notes. Even if you don't fully understand something on the first pass, your mind stores it for recall, which is why frequent reading or review increases chances of retention and comprehension.

5. **The pen is mightier than the sword.** Learn to take great notes. A by-product of our modern culture is that we have grown accustomed to getting our information in short doses. We've subconsciously trained ourselves to assimilate information into neat little packages. Messy notes fragment the flow of information. Your notes can be much clearer with proper formatting. *The Cornell Method* is one such format. This method was popularized in *How to Study in College*, Ninth Edition, by Walter Pauk. You can benefit from the method without purchasing an additional book by simply looking up the method online. Below is a sample of how *The Cornell Method* can be adapted for use with this guide.

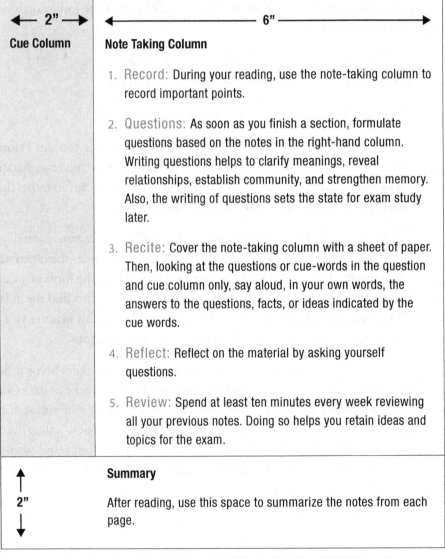

← 2" → **Cue Column**	← 6" → **Note Taking Column**
	1. Record: During your reading, use the note-taking column to record important points.
	2. Questions: As soon as you finish a section, formulate questions based on the notes in the right-hand column. Writing questions helps to clarify meanings, reveal relationships, establish community, and strengthen memory. Also, the writing of questions sets the state for exam study later.
	3. Recite: Cover the note-taking column with a sheet of paper. Then, looking at the questions or cue-words in the question and cue column only, say aloud, in your own words, the answers to the questions, facts, or ideas indicated by the cue words.
	4. Reflect: Reflect on the material by asking yourself questions.
	5. Review: Spend at least ten minutes every week reviewing all your previous notes. Doing so helps you retain ideas and topics for the exam.
↑ 2" ↓	**Summary** After reading, use this space to summarize the notes from each page.

Adapted from How to Study in College, Ninth Edition, by Walter Pauk, ©2008 Wadsworth

6. **Place yourself in exile and set the mood.** Set aside a particular place and time to study that best suits your personal needs and biorhythms. If you're a night person, burn the midnight oil. If you're a morning person set yourself up with some coffee and get to it. Make your study time and place as free from distraction as possible and surround yourself with what you need, be it silence or music. Studies have shown that music can aid in concentration, absorption, and retrieval of information. Not all music, though. Classical music is said to work best

7. **Get pointed in the right direction.** Use arrows to point to important passages or pieces of information. It's easier to read than a page full of yellow highlights. Highlighting can be used sparingly, but add an arrow to the margin to call attention to it.

8. **Check your budget.** You should at least review all the content material before your test, but allocate the most amount of time to the areas that need the most refreshing. It sounds obvious, but it's easy to forget. You can use the study rubric above to balance your study budget.

> *The proctor will write the start time where it can be seen and then, later, provide the time remaining, typically fifteen minutes before the end of the test.*

Testing Tips

1. **Get smart, play dumb.** Sometimes a question is just a question. No one is out to trick you, so don't assume that the test writer is looking for something other than what was asked. Stick to the question as written and don't overanalyze.

2. **Do a double take.** Read test questions and answer choices at least twice because it's easy to miss something, to transpose a word or some letters. If you have no idea what the correct answer is, skip it and come back later if there's time. If you're still clueless, it's okay to guess. Remember, you're scored on the number of questions you answer correctly and you're not penalized for wrong answers. The worst case scenario is that you miss a point from a good guess.

3. **Turn it on its ear.** The syntax of a question can often provide a clue, so make things interesting and turn the question into a statement to see if it changes the meaning or relates better (or worse) to the answer choices.

4. **Get out your magnifying glass.** Look for hidden clues in the questions because it's difficult to write a multiple-choice question without giving away part of the answer in the options presented. In most questions you can readily eliminate one or two potential answers, increasing your chances of answering correctly to 50/50, which will help out if you've skipped a question and gone back to it (see tip #2).

5. **Call it intuition.** Often your first instinct is correct. If you've been studying the content you've likely absorbed something and have subconsciously retained the knowledge. On questions you're not sure about trust your instincts because a first impression is usually correct.

6. **Graffiti.** Sometimes it's a good idea to mark your answers directly on the test booklet and go back to fill in the optical scan sheet later. You don't get extra points for perfectly blackened ovals. If you choose to manage your test this way, be sure not to mismark your answers when you transcribe to the scan sheet.

7. **Become a clock-watcher.** You have a set amount of time to answer the questions. Don't get bogged down laboring over a question you're not sure about when there are ten others you could answer more readily. If you choose to follow the advice of tip #2, be sure you leave time near the end to go back and fill in the scan sheet.

Do the Drill

No matter how prepared you feel it's sometimes a good idea to apply Murphy's Law. So the following tips might seem silly, mundane, or obvious, but we're including them anyway.

1. **Remember, you are what you eat, so bring a snack.** Choose from the list of energizing foods that appear earlier in the introduction.

2. **You're not too sexy for your test.** Wear comfortable clothes. You'll be distracted if your belt is too tight or if you're too cold or too hot.

3. **Lie to yourself.** Even if you think you're a prompt person, pretend you're not and leave plenty of time to get to the testing center. Map it out ahead of time and do a dry run if you have to. There's no need to add road rage to your list of anxieties.

4. **No ticket, no test.** Bring your admission ticket as well as **two** forms of identification, including one with a picture and signature. You will not be admitted to the test without these things.

5. **You can't take it with you.** Leave any study aids, dictionaries, notebooks, computers, and the like at home. Certain tests **do** allow a scientific or four-function calculator, so check ahead of time to see if your test does.

6. **Prepare for the desert.** Any time spent on a bathroom break **cannot** be made up later, so use your judgment on the amount you eat or drink.

7. Quiet, Please! Keeping your own time is a good idea, but not with a timepiece that has a loud ticker. If you use a watch, take it off and place it nearby but not so that it distracts you. And **silence your cell phone**.

To the best of our ability, we have compiled the content you need to know in this book and in the accompanying online resources. The rest is up to you. You can use the study and testing tips or you can follow your own methods. Either way, you can be confident that there aren't any missing pieces of information and there shouldn't be any surprises in the content on the test.

If you have questions about test fees, registration, electronic testing, or other content verification issues please visit *www.ets.org*.

Good luck!

Sharon Wynne
Founder, XAMonline

DOMAIN I
STUDENTS AS LEARNERS

PERSONALIZED STUDY PLAN

PERSONALIZED STUDY PLAN

			KNOWN MATERIAL/ SKIP IT
PAGE	**COMPETENCY AND SKILL**		
20	2.3	**Understands the implications and application of legislation relating to students with exceptionalities on classroom practice**	☐
	2.3.1:	Identifies the provisions of legislation relevant to students with exceptionalities, such as Americans with Disabilities Act (ADA); Individuals with Disabilities Education Act (IDEA); Section 504, Rehabilitation Act (504)	☐
	2.3.2:	Explains how the provisions of legislation relating to students with exceptionalities affect classroom practice	☐
21	2.4:	**Recognizes the traits, behaviors, and needs of intellectually gifted students**	☐
22	2.5:	**Recognizes that the process of English language acquisition affects the educational experience of English language learners (ELLs)**	☐
23	2.6:	**Knows a variety of approaches for accommodating students with exceptionalities in each phase of the education process**	☐
	2.6.1:	Recognizes students with exceptionalities require particular accommodations	☐
	2.6.2 :	Knows how to modify instruction, assessment, and communication methods to meet a recognized need	☐
25	3.1:	**Knows the major contributions of foundational behavioral theorists to education**	☐
	3.1.1:	Relates the work of behavioral theorists to educational contexts, such as Thorndike, Watson, Maslow, Skinner, Erikson	☐
27	3.2:	**Understands the implications of foundational motivation theories for instruction, learning, and classroom management**	☐
	3.2.1:	Defines terms related to foundational motivation theory, such as self-determination, attribution, extrinsic/intrinsic motivation, cognitive dissonance, classic and operant conditioning, positive and negative reinforcement	☐
	3.2.2:	Relates motivation theory to instruction, learning, and classroom management	☐
30	3.3:	**Knows principles and strategies for classroom management**	☐
	3.3.1:	Knows how to develop classroom routines and procedures	☐
	3.3.2:	Knows how to maintain accurate records	☐
	3.3.3	Knows how to establish standards of conduct	☐
	3.3.4:	Knows how to arrange classroom space	☐

PERSONALIZED STUDY PLAN

KNOWN MATERIAL/ SKIP IT

PAGE	COMPETENCY AND SKILL	
	3.3.5: Recognizes ways of promoting a positive learning environment	☐
35	**3.4: Knows a variety of strategies for helping students develop self-motivation**	☐
	3.4.1: Assigning valuable tasks	☐
	3.4.2: Providing frequent positive feedback	☐
	3.4.3: Including students in instructional decisions	☐
	3.4.4: De-emphasizing grades	☐

COMPETENCY 1
STUDENTS DEVELOPMENT AND THE LEARNING PROCESS

SKILL 1.1	Understands the theoretical foundations of how students learn

SKILL 1.1.1	Knows how knowledge is constructed

SKILL 1.1.2	Knows a variety of means by which skills are acquired

As a teacher, you will have the opportunity to instruct in a variety of ways. Using as many ways as possible, called **differentiated instruction**, is a key way of reaching children with multiple learning styles.

So, how is knowledge constructed? How are skills acquired?

Learning begins in infancy. Babies are exposed to multiple stimuli in their environment, and for years beginning in babyhood, they learn what is often repeated. This creates a background schema, which is a mental file cabinet in which all known information is stored for later retrieval. When a child learns something new, she reaches toward her background schema to help her make sense of new information. For example, if she is learning about patterns, she may connect this new concept to a time when she matched colors. With her teacher's help, she will be able to make the leap from matching colors to finding a pattern. Lev Vygotsky, a constructivist educational philosopher, referred to the zone of proximal development. This is the area between what a child can do on her own and what a child can do with a teacher's assistance. Eventually, the child will be able to move on to the next level on her own. Other constructivist theorists, such as Jean Piaget and John Dewey, argued that experiences and social environments help form knowledge. Piaget created stages of cognitive development, which will we learn in detail in the next skill. These stages define what a child can learn at each point in his development. When a teacher understands these stages, she can adjust instruction to match what a student needs.

Lev Vygotsky, a constructivist educational philosopher, referred to the zone of proximal development.

So how does a child construct knowledge?

- Experience
- Background schema
- Zone of proximal development

Understands a variety of cognitive processes and how they are developed

What do cognitive processes look like? How are they developed?

As previously discussed, knowledge comes from experience and sociocultural influences. When a child connects familiar knowledge to new knowledge, he is making new connections and adding to his background schema. As children get older, they become metacognitive. Metacognition is when a person is aware of how she learns, what her cognitive processes look like, and how she uses her cognitive skills to learn a new concept. For example, an older student may know that she is a visual learner, so she will take notes during every lecture to give herself a chance to remember the material. In the next section, we will talk in depth about well-known educational philosophers who laid the foundation for today's schools.

Knows the major contributions of foundational theorists to education

Relates the work of theorists to educational contexts, such as Bandura, Bruner, Dewey, Piaget, Vygotsky, Kohlberg, Bloom

There are many educational philosophers, many of whom we will discuss in this study guide, but the foundational theorists are Bandura, Bruner, Dewey, Piaget, Vygotsky, Kohlberg, and Bloom. Each philosopher falls into various categories of theory, and each created measurements that teachers continue to use to assess student progress.

Vygotsky

Lev Vygotsky, a sociocultural, constructivist theorist who wrote in the early 1900s but was not known to the West until the 1960s, argued that learning is interactive and that interactions are key to development. His social development theory asserts that social understanding comes before individual growth. Additionally, children learn from what he called MKOs, or more knowledgeable others. These are usually adults, but they can be peers who have a stronger understanding of a concept and can coach or teach a new learner. Children will learn about culture and sociocultural contexts from working together and learning from one another, as well as being coached through their ZPD, or zone of proximal development. The zone of proximal development refers to the space between independence in a skill and needing help to finish a task. Often, the coaching is done by an MKO. Eventually, the student will learn the concept and be able to complete the task independently.

This doesn't mean a teacher should just allow students to learn from one another or have a chaotic classroom. It just means that she should act as a facilitator, not a lecturer. She should embrace her students' roles in teaching and helping one another. Additionally, she plays a strong role in the zone of proximal development. A teacher will help students move from one level to the next.

Dewey

John Dewey, published in the early to mid-1900s, fundamentally changed ideas behind education when he argued that learning should be authentic (meaningful to a child's context) and not just rote memorization. Children should not be passive learners, but should learn by doing and learn skills that will serve them well in life. John Dewey believed that as teachers, we are preparing children to be acting members of society, and a strong classroom community will be an excellent starting point.

Piaget

Constructivist theorist Jean Piaget (translated to English in 1955), argued that knowledge is constructed through four developmental stages. These stages measure intellectual and cognitive development, and much of today's education and parenting advice is based on Piaget's stages. Not every adult will make it through the fourth stage, but these are general guidelines for the stages through which most people will travel during their most intense years of growth. The first stage begins in infancy, and it is called the sensorimotor stage. A child is in the sensorimotor stage from birth to age two. Features of this stage include learning through simple motor and sensory responses. Children of this age have limited movement, so much of what they experience will come through their sight, sound, touch, and, as they become a little older, what they can travel to see. This is often why an infant or toddler will explore something new by placing it in his mouth. He is learning through the senses of touch and taste, two of his five senses.

The next stage, the preoperational stage, is evident in children from ages two through seven. Features of this stage include a large jump in vocabulary and expressive and receptive language development. Piaget asserted that children in this stage are egocentric and view the world simply through their own lens. They cannot see things from other points of views and cannot understand concrete logic. There have been criticisms of this point of view; other philosophers have said that children as young as four can see situations from others' points of view and can be sympathetic toward others.

The next stage, the concrete operational stage, is evident in children from ages 7 to 11. Features of this stage include the ability to think logically about situations, specifically to use inductive logic. Inductive logic is the ability to generalize a specific experience into a more general category. Children of this age do not yet have the ability to think in the abstract or hypothetical; their skills are focused on concrete thinking.

The last stage, the formal operational stage, is evident in children from age 12 through adulthood. This is the period of development when people learn how to think in the abstract and use deductive reasoning. Deductive reasoning is the ability to take a general idea and use the hypothetical to make an educated guess about a future outcome. This stage requires much abstract thought, planning, and strategizing. A child will pull not only from her own background schema but also from hypotheticals to come to a solution.

Kohlberg

Lawrence Kohlberg extended Piaget's theory. Kohlberg, who published in the late 1950s, argued that moral development is more detailed than Piaget asserted and that it takes the entire life, not just childhood, to attain all the levels. The first level is named preconventional morality, and is, like the other stages, broken down into sub-stages. The first sub-stage is called obedience and punishment. Especially prevalent in young children, a person who obeys rules does so because he is trying to avoid the punishment. For example, when you say to a two-year-old, "don't hit or you have to sit in time out," the child stops hitting because he doesn't want to sit in time out, not because he understand that hitting hurts and isn't nice. During the next sub-stage of level one, individualism and exchange, children see different points of view and can see how an action would affect a specific individual.

The next level is conventional morality, and this also has two stages. The first is the interpersonal relationships stage. In this stage, a person is very focused on what society expects of him and will want to live up to those expectations. He often thinks about how his choices will affect others. In the next stage, maintaining social order, a person moves from thinking about the individual to thinking about society. How will a choice affect a group of people? Rules are in place for a reason, and members of society have a duty to maintain that social order.

In the third level, postconventional morality, a person's thinking becomes abstract. In the first stage of this level, social contract and individual rights, a person understands that different members of society have different beliefs and opinions. The person understands that rules are necessary for society, and the idea of democracy and agreeing on these rules is a feature of this stage. In the last stage, universal principles, a person moves toward complete abstract principles and gray areas. A person understands that there are rules to society but has also created her own set of internal rules, which may conflict with society's rules.

Bruner

Jerome Bruner, who published in the early 1960s, is another well-known cognitive theorist. He agreed with Vygotsky's argument that learning comes from previous knowledge and argued that new ideas are constructed from familiar ones, or background schema. Bruner believed that the role of the teacher is to meet a child where he is and facilitate him into the next phase, much like Vygotsky's zone of proximal development. A child should be ready to learn the material the teacher is presenting, the material should be built upon prior knowledge, and the teacher should use instructional time to close any cognitive gaps in the child's learning.

Bloom

Benjamin Bloom, who published in the 1950s and 1960s, created a taxonomy with which to categorize cognitive understanding. Teachers use this taxonomy every day in creating lesson plans and assessments. Each category of the taxonomy represents a certain skill level and understanding. The taxonomy is shaped like a pyramid, with the easiest category at the bottom and the one that is the most difficult to attain at the top. It looks like this:

Benjamin Bloom, who published in the 1950s and 1960s, created a taxonomy with which to categorize cognitive understanding.

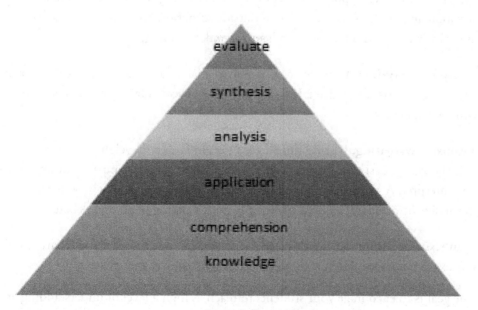

Bloom's first taxonomy

Recently, the taxonomy was revised to use verbs instead of nouns and to rearrange the top two cognitive stages of understanding. The new version looks like this:

Knowledge = Remembering

Comprehension = Understanding

Application = Applying

Analysis = Analyzing

Synthesis = Creating (top level)

Evaluation = Evaluating (below Creating)

Now that you know the terms of Bloom's taxonomy, what will each of these terms mean to you as an instructor? You need to know what each stage means for each student.

Knowledge/Remembering: This is the most basic level of understanding. Can a student recite facts? Define terms? If so, she has basic knowledge.

Comprehension/Understanding: Can a student explain a concrete concept in her own words? Can she explain, predict, infer, or give an example of a concept? If so, she has comprehended a concept.

Application/Applying: Application is the first more abstract stage of understanding. A child who can apply a concept can use her background schema in a new situation and apply this knowledge to outside scenarios. She can predict, solve, and construct based on her more advanced understanding.

Analysis/Analyzing: A student who is able to analyze a concept can break it down into smaller parts, recognize errors, distinguish between a fact and inference, and compare concepts.

Evaluate/Evaluating: During this stage, a person is able to weigh various options and choose the best one. He can evaluate, explain, contrast, compare, summarize, and interpret. A student could demonstrate the ability to evaluate by writing a persuasive or compare/contrast paper or by participating in an oral debate.

Synthesis/Creating: During this stage, a person can put together small parts to create a general idea. He can combine, explain, organize, and create.

The goal is to encourage your students to reach as high a level of understanding as possible in each concept. Younger students may be able to reach only lower levels of understanding, but as a student gets older, he will be able to learn concepts in more abstract ways and apply them in a more mature setting.

Bandura

Albert Bandura, who published his social learning theory in 1977, is often called a combination between a behaviorist and a cognitive theorist. His theories involve a child's ability to pay attention, remember, and be motivated to learn. He argued that there are four ways to learn: from one another, through observation, through imitation, and through modeling. Bandura is also responsible for the self-efficacy theory, which states that a person's perception of his capabilities is a form of positive thinking that involves a person believing that he can accomplish certain goals.

> **SKILL 1.3** Understands the concepts and terms related to a variety of learning theories, such as metacognition, schema, transfer, self-efficacy, self-regulation, zone of proximal development, classical and operant conditioning

Learning theorists use various terms to define their concepts, and it is important to become familiar with each of their terms and the person who is responsible for its usage. Some we have already briefly discussed but will analyze further in this section.

Metacognition: A person who is metacognitive knows his own learning style and how he learns. He understands his ability, what he can understand, and what he needs to learn a new concept. This is a skill with which a teacher can help a child, and one that will become more comfortable for a child as she grows.

Schema: How does a person learn new information? By reaching into his background schema—his mental files—and finding familiar information that matches the new information. For example, a student who is learning multiplication will use his knowledge about addition to understand the leap between addition and multiplication. Students come to school with background schema from their home literacies and sociocultural backgrounds. A strong teacher will identify this prior knowledge and use it to leap forward into new knowledge.

Transfer: Transfer is a similar concept to background schema. Whereas background schema refers to the knowledge a student brings to a new concept, transfer

> **METACOGNITION:** A person who is metacognitive knows his own learning style and how he learns. He understands his ability, what he can understand, and what he needs to learn a new concept. This is a skill with which a teacher can help a child, and one that will become more comfortable for a child as she grows.

refers to a student's ability to connect one concept to another similar concept. For example, if a student plays the guitar, she may be able to transfer some of that knowledge to learning piano. She will be able to recognize the common features in both skill sets and connect two concepts. Sometimes a child will incorrectly determine that two concepts have common features and will need help moving toward a more correct idea.

Self-efficacy: We have spoken about self-efficacy in Skill 1.2, but as a brief overview, self-efficacy is part of Bandura's social cognitive theory and explains a person's belief that he can or cannot accomplish a goal. A person who has strong self-efficacy will accomplish goals, whereas a person without it may not. It is a similar concept to self-confidence.

Self-regulation: Self-regulation is a skill with which very young children struggle. Children become better at recognizing this trait as they get older. Can a child control his impulses? Can he patiently wait his turn? Can he independently wait until it is his turn? Can he choose one action over another because he knows the consequences of each and has weighed them? If so, he has good self-regulation. Toddlers and preschoolers struggle with this skill because they are not yet able to understand consequences of actions or control their own impulses for very long.

Zone of proximal development (ZPD): We have talked about ZPD in Skill 1.2, but a brief overview follows. ZPD is part of Vygotsky's sociocultural theory, and it explains the gap between what a child can do independently and the skills with which he needs instructor assistance. A teacher will help his student move from needing help understanding a term to being able to handle the concept independently.

Classical and operant conditioning: These terms were made famous by Pavlov, whom you may associate with the famous "Pavlov's dogs." Through his experiments, Pavlov learned that at the signal of a bell, given right before meals, his dogs would salivate, expecting to be fed. Over time, they would salivate just at the sound of the bell, without seeing the food. This theory of using a neutral stimulus to generate an automatic response is termed classical conditioning. In contrast, operant conditioning is when a reward or punishment is given after a specific behavior. Classical conditioning focuses on involuntary behaviors (such as salivating), while operational conditioning focuses on voluntary behaviors (such as a classroom incentive for turning in homework).

> **SKILL 1.4** **Knows the distinguishing characteristics of the stages in each domain of human development (i.e., cognitive, physical, social, and moral)**

> **SKILL 1.4.1** **Describes the characteristics of a typical child in each stage and each domain**

Cognitive: The major theorist behind cognitive development is Piaget. We spoke in depth about his four stages of cognitive development in Skill 1.2. To briefly summarize, each stage explains the type of thinking of which a child is capable at any particular point in growth. Often these classifications set the stage for teachers' lesson plans and assessments. Although Piaget has met with some criticism, he is well known as a foundational theorist of cognitive development.

Physical: The first two years of human development is instrumental in physical growth. In the first few months, a child learns to roll over. Next, he sits up on his own around six months. Most children will crawl in the second half of the first year, although some babies skip this stage entirely! He will then learn to pull himself up to standing and cruise around furniture. In this stage, he will hold onto chairs or couches as he moves sideways around a room. Eventually, between about 11 and 16 months, he will learn to walk. Next, he will run and climb, and by age two and a half he will be able to jump off the ground, even though he will have been trying for months prior to succeeding. In the preschool years, he will get stronger; he will run faster, climb more, and become much more fluid in his movements. If he is practicing sports or is involved in regular physical activity, he will get stronger and more confident in his movements. A child who is not meeting his physical milestones in the later part of the developmental window may be evaluated by a pediatrician to see if there are any developmental delays or if extra therapy is needed to help the child progress.

A three- to five-year-old will be working on gross and fine motor skills, as they are developing rapidly. Children this age learn how to kick balls, throw and catch, and use crayons, scissors, and glue, and they begin working on writing letters. A dominant hand may emerge. By the time a child turns 5 or 6, he is beginning to perfect these skills, all the way up to age 12. Children become proficient at athletics, balancing, writing with pencils and pens, typing on computers, and working with screens.

Social: How does a child interact with others? How do children control their impulses and emotions? How do they handle disappointment, sharing, sympathy, and empathy, and how do they maintain friendships? Can they identify their own feelings? These are all measures of social development.

SKILL 1.4.2 Recognizes typical and atypical variance within each stage and each domain

Infants are too young to talk, but they exhibit emotional development very early. They cry when the feel unsafe, hungry, or tired, and as early as six weeks, they show a social smile to their caregiver. Bonding with a caregiver is key to an infant's social development. She has to feel safe to understand what is socially expected of her. When her life is predictable and her caregiver is responsive, she will be more apt to develop socially.

When an infant starts to babble in the second half of the first year, she is responding to social cues of the people around her by trying to converse in the only way she knows. She will learn her first words based on what is said to her often.

Toddlers struggle with social cues. Sharing is difficult for them, as is identifying their feelings. This is why a toddler will throw tantrums and fall to pieces when he doesn't get his way. He doesn't have the language or the social skills to identify what he is feeling and how to get what he wants or needs. As he gets older and gains more verbal skills and maturity, he will understand the concepts of taking turns, being someone's friend, and showing sympathy for others. Adult relationships continue to be critical to a child's social development. As with physical development, if a child is not showing social cues at appropriate times or at the end of the developmental window, he may be evaluated by a physical or child psychologist to see if extra therapy is needed to aide in social development. For example, some young children may struggle with eye contact, may not understand social cues in terms of making friends, or may struggle with conversing with children their own age. Sometimes, professional intervention will be necessary.

As a child grows, her relationship with family members and teachers will aide in her social development. She will learn from those around her, as evident in sociocultural theory, and bring these literacies to other aspects of learning. Erik Erikson is a critical theorist in social development, and we will cover him in depth later in the study guide.

Sources

Social-emotional development domain
http://www.cde.ca.gov/sp/cd/re/itf09soce
modev.asp
Retrieved Oct. 26, 2014.

Stages of intellectual development in children and teenagers
http://childdevelopmentinfo.com/child
development/piaget/
Retrieved Oct. 26, 2014.

SKILL 1.5 Understands how learning theory and human development impact the instructional process

> SKILL
> 1.5.1
> **Defines the relationship between learning theory and human development**

> SKILL
> 1.5.2
> **Provides examples of how learning theory is impacted by human development**

Learning theory and human development are strongly linked. We have talked about sociocultural learning theories (that learning is tied to social interactions and observations) and cognitive learning theories (that learning is based upon various cognitive stages a child goes through as he ages). The theorists who have been discussed, such as Bandura, Piaget, Vygotsky, Kohlberg, and Bruner, all contribute critical ideas for the successful teacher. For example, if a teacher knows which of Piaget's cognitive stages her student is in, she will know how his mind is developing in that moment. If he is between the ages of 7 and 11 and is in the concrete operational stage, he will be able to sort ideas based on more than one quality, something he could not do previously. He will also be able to think in abstract terms and create logical explanations for experiences. That could be why an elementary school student is a master storyteller, always trying to tell someone about an experience she has had!

Another example is Kohlberg's moral development chart. Teachers need to understand what students are struggling with morally so they can understand how a student will look at a problem. For example, a young child is learning how to cooperate with others and how to be an appropriate leader and follower in certain social situations. This explains why kindergarteners argue often over who should play with what toy, but by first grade this argument occurs less frequently. At this point, the child is on her way to a new stage. Kohlberg's theories also can explain why some students may seem to be behind others in social development. Perhaps they are on the tail end of one stage while others have moved to the next stage. discovering information.

> SKILL
> 1.5.3
> **Uses knowledge of learning theory to solve educational problems**

> SKILL
> 1.5.4
> **Uses knowledge of human development to solve educational problems**

An educator has to understand that all these theories—cognitive, moral, and social—come together to create a child's development. Engaging lessons are those that match students' levels of cognitive, moral, and social development. You would also not ask a preschooler to determine how his actions will affect society as a whole; he is too early in his moral development, according to Kohlberg, to be able to make such a sophisticated distinction.

An educator has to understand that all these theories—cognitive, moral, and social—come together to create a child's development.

COMPETENCY 2
STUDENTS AS DIVERSE LEARNERS

> **SKILL 2.1** Understands that a number of variables affect how individual students learn and perform

> **SKILL 2.1.1** Identifies a number of variables that affect how students learn and perform
> - learning style
> - gender
> - culture
> - socioeconomic status
> - prior knowledge and experience
> - motivation
> - self-confidence, self-esteem
> - cognitive development
> - maturity
> - language

> **SKILL 2.1.2** Provides examples of how variables might affect how students learn and perform

Learning Style: According to Howard Gardner, all children learn differently. Some students learn through visual aids such as presentations and posters, and others learn through auditory lessons such as storytelling. Some students learn kinesthetically (with their bodies), and others learn through cooperative learning and other interpersonal activities. Teachers must differentiate instruction and create lessons that encourage various learning styles so that each student has the opportunity to learn in various ways.

Gender: The following statements are an overview of learning differences based on gender. Keep in mind that they will not hold true for all boys and all girls. Girls often will enjoy sitting quietly and coloring, writing, and drawing at an early age. Often, girls will have stronger fine motor skills than boys of the same age, but boys may have stronger gross motor skills. Additionally, girls may have stronger organizational skills than boys. Boys generally are more kinesthetic; girls often have an easier time siting quietly through a visual presentation. Both genders need support, confidence-building activities, and engaging and challenging lessons.

Prior Knowledge and Experience: A teacher should begin each new lesson by measuring her students' previous knowledge and activating their background schema. When a child can pull his familiar knowledge into a new concept, he will have a much easier time moving into a higher level of understanding because he will know where the new information "fits." A teacher can activate prior knowledge through KWL charts, an informal class discussion, a journal entry, or even a pretest.

Language/Culture: Gloria Ladson-Billings refers to a culturally responsive classroom, in which teachers create a connection between academic lessons and home life to make lessons relevant to students' cultures when appropriate. For example, when beginning a unit, a teacher will ask his students about their background knowledge on a subject area. At this point, it would be appropriate for students to share culturally relevant stories to help connect the new concept to something that is more familiar. Additionally, be aware that some parents may not be native English speakers, so, if possible, have newsletters and communications available in a family's primary language.

Socioeconomic Status: A teacher needs to be cognizant of Maslow's hierarchy of needs. For example, a student who is worried about his basic needs, such as food, shelter, and heat, most likely will not be interested in reading books or working on math. He may be hungry, self-conscious because his clothes are dirty, or cold from another night spent in a house with no heat. Alternatively, a student who comes from a well-off family may be under immense pressure to succeed, and this can cause anxiety or depression. Just as a teacher is aware of her students' cultural backgrounds, she also must be aware of her students' socioeconomic status and be sensitive to their needs. Don't ask students to purchase materials for class projects, and, especially in the lower grades, don't require students to spend time outside school hours on cooperative learning projects. Be aware that schedules may prevent eager parents from participating in school activities, and some parents who may want to attend may not have a car, or even a phone. Try to include as many parents as possible in school activities by scheduling activities at varying times, using several mediums to communicate, and even offering incentives, if necessary.

Motivation: The more motivation a child has to succeed, the more success she will have in school. Motivation can be extrinsic or intrinsic, and whether a student is extrinsically or intrinsically motivated depends on the student's maturity level, cognitive development level, and age. For example, a high school student will be more likely to understand that learning is important to be successful in life than a younger student, who may do his homework only to avoid consequences or receive a reward promised by a teacher or parent. If a teacher knows her class needs to be extrinsically motivated to succeed, a token economy or reward system can be successful.

Cognitive Development: Jean Piaget asserted that everyone goes through four major stages of cognitive development. These stages (see Skill 1.2) discuss how a person grows in intelligence throughout his life and which concepts will be clear and confusing to him as he matures. Teachers who are aware of these stages can have high expectations for their students, and they also will know their students' limits.

Self-Confidence/Self-Esteem/Maturity: A teacher should spend a large amount of time building his students' self-confidence. He can do this by creating a safe and nurturing environment in which everyone feels comfortable sharing, having personal conferences with students, creating lessons that engage students with various learning styles, and finding each student's path to success. Some students will struggle to succeed in the traditional way, and the teacher must make these children feel that their abilities are useful and important. Maturity also can be a factor in student success. Some students who misbehave—for example, struggling with the rules of a classroom and having trouble sitting still, listening, and following directions—also will have trouble academically. Often, these students do well with visual behavior charts, constant but gentle reminders, and extrinsic motivators.

SKILL 2.2	Recognizes areas of exceptionality and their potential impact on student learning

SKILL 2.2.1	Identifies areas of exceptionality, such as cognitive, auditory, visual, motor/physical, speech/language, behavioral

Exceptional learners, or students who have IEPs or who are labeled as gifted and talented, will fall into one or more of several categories. These students will need to be treated with their specific needs in mind. According to the Center for Parent Information and Resources, exceptional students may fall into the following categories:

A. **Autism:** A disability affecting verbal and nonverbal communication, social skills, and ability to function well in a classroom environment.

B. **Deaf/blind:** Difficulty seeing and hearing, making communication quite difficult.

C. **Developmental delay:** A delay in a crucial developmental area such as cognition, physicality, or behavior.

D. **Hearing impairment:** Difficulty hearing.

E. **Multiple disabilities:** When many of these categories are present.

F. **Intellectual disability:** Very intense below-average intellectual functioning.

G. **Learning disability:** A disorder that specifically affects a basic learning skill such as reading, writing, spelling, or math.

H. **Orthopedic impairment:** A severe impairment of the body that affects learning.

I. **Other health impairment:** Limited strength that results in limited alertness and success in the academic environment.

J. **Serious emotional disturbance**: Inability or intense difficulty creating or maintaining relationships; difficulty "feeling normal"; volatile, roller coaster feelings; strong fears; or difficulty learning that cannot be explained by other factors.

K. **Speech or language impairment:** Communication disorder such as speech, stuttering, or language or voice impairment.

L. **Traumatic brain injury:** A brain injury caused by force or trauma to the head that has adversely affected learning. Students may have trouble with problem solving, memory, speech, or abstract thinking.

M. **Visual impairment:** Difficulty with vision that adversely affects learning.

SKILL 2.2.2 **Explains a variety of ways exceptionalities may impact student learning**

As noted, identification within one or more of these categories can have major effects on a student's ability to learn in a typical classroom. Therefore, IEPs and accommodations will be crucial in allowing all children to succeed. For example, a student with a visual impairment may need larger print, or braille. A child with autism may need access to a sensory room to calm down, a personal instructional aide to help with communication, or items in the classroom that he can use to prevent sensory overload. Teachers must be aware of their students and follow their IEP accordingly, creating options for exceptional students so everyone is set up for success.

Categories of disability under IDEA. Retrieved from: http://www.parentcenterhub.org/repository/categories/

> **SKILL 2.3** Understands the implications and application of legislation relating to students with exceptionalities on classroom practice

> **SKILL 2.3.1** Identifies the provisions of legislation relevant to students with exceptionalities, such as Americans with Disabilities Act (ADA); Individuals with Disabilities Education Act (IDEA); Section 504, Rehabilitation Act (504)

As an educator, you are going to be extremely familiar with legislation that helps and gives opportunities to your students. It is important to understand three major laws; ADA, IDEA, and Section 504, which are examined below.

Americans with Disabilities Act (ADA): The Americans with Disabilities Act was passed in 1990 as a civil rights act. It protects all citizens against discrimination based on a disability.

For example, a person who is blind cannot be denied a job due to his inability to see. This law protects any person with a documented physical or mental disability. Of course, it also recognizes that a person might be denied a job due to lack of skill, and that is acceptable.

Individuals with Disabilities Education Act (IDEA): Passed in 1997 and amended in 2004, IDEA is an education bill that protects children from ages 3 to 21. This law gives financial aid to ensure education services are available for children with documented disabilities.

A child who falls under IDEA may have autism, emotional disturbance, physical impairments such as deafness or deaf-blindness, orthopedic impairments, speech impairments, or brain injury. The state is required under law to provide a Free and Appropriate Public Education (FAPE) to these students.

Section 504: This law falls under civil rights, like the ADA, and affects any person who has a documented disability that substantially affects day-to-day activities, such as walking, learning, breathing, or eating. No one with a documented disability can be denied acceptance into programs that receive federal financial assistance because of their disability.

> **AMERICANS WITH DISABILITIES ACT (ADA):** The Americans with Disabilities Act was passed in 1990 as a civil rights act. It protects all citizens against discrimination based on a disability.

> **INDIVIDUALS WITH DISABILITIES EDUCATION ACT (IDEA):** Passed in 1997 and amended in 2004, IDEA is an education bill that protects children from ages 3 to 21. This law gives financial aid to ensure education services are available for children with documented disabilities.

> **SKILL 2.3.2** Explains how the provisions of legislation relating to students with exceptionalities affect classroom practice

When will you need knowledge of these laws? You may sit as the classroom teacher at an Individualized Education Plan (IEP) meeting, where you will give opinions on the student's progress and challenges. Knowledge of these laws will give you an idea of what the student's disability means, what types of services he is offered, and the responsibility of the school to provide the appropriate and least-restrictive education.

Additionally, classroom practice will be affected daily as you follow these laws the classroom. For example, a student who needs occupational, physical, or speech therapy will need to leave the classroom to receive these extra services, which will be paid for by the state under IDEA. As a classroom teacher, you need to have accommodations to encourage each student. If you have a student who is blind, you may have books in braille. If you have a student who is autistic, you may have the opportunity to send her to a sensory room for a sensory break when she is feeling overwhelmed or overstimulated. These options are provided by the laws that mandate a free and appropriate public education for each child. As a classroom teacher, you will most likely work with the special education teacher, the child's parent, and perhaps a guidance counselor or administrator to put in place a successful plan for each child who needs one.

http://dredf.org/advocacy/comparison.html Retrieved Oct. 28, 2014.

> **SECTION 504:** This law falls under civil rights, like the ADA, and affects any person who has a documented disability that substantially affects day-to-day activities, such as walking, learning, breathing, or eating. No one with a documented disability can be denied acceptance into programs that receive federal financial assistance because of their disability.

SKILL 2.4 Recognizes the traits, behaviors, and needs of intellectually gifted students

Gifted students are those whose ability and achievement level are extremely high. Often, signs of giftedness can start in infancy. Gifted babies may be aware of their surroundings earlier, may speak earlier, may show interest in early literacy well before their peers, or may show giftedness in spatial awareness like building.

But in school, gifted students will show other unique characteristics. According to the National Society for the Gifted and Talented, traits may include "perfectionism, heightened sensitivity to their own expectations, problem solving minds, abstract thinkers, identify success with only the grade of 'A,' and may have one super talent in one or two areas such as leadership, visual/performing arts, creative thinking or a specific academic ability" (http://www.nsgt.org/giftedness-defined/). These students may also learn to read early, have an advanced vocabulary, make unique conceptual connections, and be very curious. However, they may get bored quickly with rote tasks such as worksheets or drill homework. In fact, they may not even complete it, and sometimes parents of gifted students may be told that their child is often off task, not engaged, or a behavior problem. Often, that is because gifted children struggle with material that is too easy or that they can master quickly. A gifted child also may struggle socially, and this may be evident in the classroom.

> *Gifted students will show other unique characteristics. According to the National Society for the Gifted and Talented, traits may include "perfectionism, heightened sensitivity to their own expectations, problem solving minds, abstract thinkers, identify success with only the grade of 'A,' and may have one super talent in one or two areas such as leadership, visual/performing arts, creative thinking or a specific academic ability" (http://www.nsgt.org/giftedness-defined/).*

Gifted students' needs are going to be distinctive, because their talents are diverse and unique. It's important, first of all, to meet their academic needs. Often, a regular curriculum is going to be boring for them, and they may act out as a result. Therefore, it is critical to find activities that are engaging for them. These often include problem solving or self-directed learning. Authentic projects that get students involved in the community, use multisensory learning, use teachers as facilitators, or use technology—in general, work that goes beyond the textbook—is key. Gifted students are often intrinsically motivated, but they also want to be included in the direction of their learning. They may struggle with group work, because they already know the direction in which they want to take the project. This doesn't mean they shouldn't be part of cooperative learning; quite the opposite. Although it can be frustrating, this is the perfect opportunity to teach this type of student how to listen to and include others. Work on communication techniques, small-group skills, and communication skills while preparing students to work in groups. Some gifted students may appear to be emotionally needy or perfectionists, or they may have difficulties in social situations. Just because they are beyond their peers in one area doesn't mean they may not need help in others. Teachers must be patient with this group of students, just as they would with any other group.

Often, gifted students have the opportunity be pulled out of class and put into a homogenous group (others who learn similarly) so they can challenge one another and feel satisfied with their learning. Often these groups will have self-directed lessons such as literature groups, math challenges, or science fairs. Additionally, Socratic questioning works well, because it invites the student to move forward with his own thinking. The teacher acts as facilitator, answering questions with other questions.

> **SKILL 2.5** Recognizes that the process of English language acquisition affects the educational experience of English language learners (ELLs)

It is important for ELL teachers to engage learners in what Gloria Ladson-Billings calls a **culturally responsive classroom**. In this type of classroom, the students are looked at holistically—not just as ELL learners, but as students with a rich and distinctive culture and unique home literacies. The teacher should use student backgrounds as schema and prior knowledge to connect them to the state standards. She will ask them for their own knowledge and experiences and bridge the curriculum in ways her students will understand, based on their own cultures. Giving her students ownership over the curriculum will create a sense of pride, respect, and, ultimately, success.

SKILL 2.6 Knows a variety of approaches for accommodating students with exceptionalities in each phase of the education process

SKILL 2.6.1 Recognizes students with exceptionalities require particular accommodations

Exceptionalities means differences. Many students will have differences that require accommodations. Some will be more obvious than others. For example, a student who is blind will need accommodations for reading and writing. A student in a wheelchair will need a ramp and elevators to reach the second level of a school. However, some accommodations will not be as obvious, and some will not be easy for the teacher alone to accommodate. It is okay and important to ask for help from special education teachers, school therapists, and administration to make these accommodations happen. For example, a student with sensory issues may need a place to go to calm down when he feels overloaded. Perhaps the librarian would offer her room as a respite. A gifted student may need extra emotional support as he battles his perfectionism against finding new material challenging. While the classroom teacher can provide this support, perhaps she has an instructional assistant who can be of help as well.

These accommodations can often be found in a student's IEP and would have been discussed formally at an IEP meeting. However, some students who are not identified as exceptional or do not have an IEP may still need accommodations. Slowing down or speeding up instruction, using differentiation, using multisensory methods, and providing opportunities for check-ins with each student can give the teacher an idea of what is working for each child.

SKILL 2.6.2 Knows how to modify instruction, assessment, and communication methods to meet a recognized need

Instruction: Differentiation and multisensory instruction are key in any classroom. Beyond that, some students may have specific needs that require modifications in instruction. Some classrooms will have an instructional assistant who will work on keeping a student on task, helping him take notes, writing down assignments, or organizing his work. Educators need to be aware of student challenges and find a way to help them understand the concepts every day.

Assessment: Assessments can be modified based on IEP accommodations. Some students may require extra time or read-alouds; some may need to take the test in small groups; and others may need frequent breaks to help keep focus. Some students who struggle with reading may need the questions and answers read aloud so their difficulty with phonics does not interrupt their knowledge of the assessment. Other students may need extended time or small groups because of difficulty paying attention.

Some students may require sensory adjustments, such as taking a test on a sensory ball, playing with a sensory toy, or even testing in a room with soft lighting.

Communication methods: Speak clearly and succinctly when giving instructions to students. Provide instructions in as many ways as possible—through visual and auditory instruction and even, when appropriate, through muscle memory! Also leave written instructions when appropriate.

Be aware of any language barriers in the class, and if possible, provide instructions in alternate languages. If that is not possible, colorful pictures can be very useful.

Use diverse communication methods when speaking to parents as well. Send home letters and emails and use the phone, pick up and drop off, and conferences to chat with parents. Additionally, try to provide school/home communication in alternative languages if possible, so parents whose primary language is not English can be part of the process and feel included.

Communication methods: Speak clearly and succinctly when giving instructions to students. Provide instructions in as many ways as possible—through visual and auditory instruction and even, when appropriate, through muscle memory! Also leave written instructions when appropriate.

COMPETENCY 3
STUDENT MOTIVATION AND LEARNING ENVIRONMENT

> **SKILL 3.1** Knows the major contributions of foundational behavioral theorists to education

> **SKILL 3.1.1** Relates the work of behavioral theorists to educational contexts, such as Thorndike, Watson, Maslow, Skinner, Erikson

When we want to motivate our students to learn, we first must understand what will make them want to learn. Various foundational behavioral theorists have given us clues as to what students needs to learn, how they learn, and what educators can do to make them progress in a more linear way. Keep these basic concepts in mind when thinking of each theorist.

Maslow: Maslow was a motivation theorist who created a well-known hierarchy of needs that explains what students need, including how they need to feel safe to learn. His hierarchy of needs is in the shape of a pyramid. The largest and most important needs, which are physiological, are at the base of the pyramid, and they includes basic needs such as food, shelter, water, and sleep. If a child is deprived of any of these, he will never move beyond this part of the pyramid. Why would a child who is starving want to learn math? It will not be on his priority list! The next level up on the pyramid is safety, and it includes the security of a person's environment. Is this space safe? Does it have the proper resources? Is it clean?

The middle layer of the pyramid, belongingness, refers to social factors such as love, friendship, and family. Up one level is esteem, which refers to achievement and confidence. Finally, the top, smallest level of the pyramid is self-actualization, and refers to morality and creativity. Each of the lower levels must be satisfied for a person to move to the next level. According to Maslow, a person will not be able to enjoy strong self-esteem and confidence until he has mastered the first three levels on the pyramid. It's important for teachers to recognize this pyramid, because often students cannot be motivated to succeed in school until their first three levels are met. A teacher needs to be sure that the child is fed, safe, warm, and loved before she tries to move forward in any curriculum.

Erik Erikson: Erikson created eight developmental stages that trace a psychosocial line of development. Over a person's entire life, he will go through these stages, during which he will struggle with one concept over another. If he succeeds in going through each stage and creates a strong relationship with the "virtue" he is learning, he will be ready to move on to the next phase. If he doesn't, he will feel negative feelings such as bitterness, shame, or resentment.

> **MASLOW:** Maslow was a motivation theorist who created a well-known hierarchy of needs that explains what students need, including how they need to feel safe to learn. His hierarchy of needs is in the shape of a pyramid. The largest and most important needs, which are physiological, are at the base of the pyramid, and they includes basic needs such as food, shelter, water, and sleep

> *The middle layer of the pyramid, belongingness, refers to social factors such as love, friendship, and family. Up one level is esteem, which refers to achievement and confidence. Finally, the top, smallest level of the pyramid is self-actualization, and refers to morality and creativity.*

> *Erikson created eight developmental stages that trace a psychosocial line of development.*

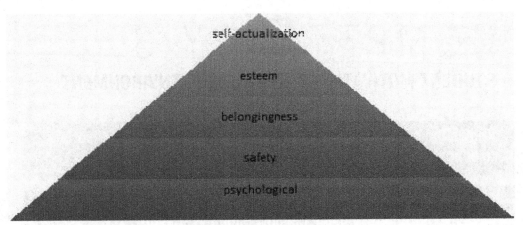

Maslow's Hierarchy of Needs

Erik Erikson's Psychosocial Stages

John Watson: In terms of behaviorists, one must start with John Watson, who published in the 1920s, and coined the term behaviorism. This term means that nurture (as opposed to nature) is responsible for creating a person's strengths and weaknesses. Watson believed that through conditioning, a person can be trained to do and succeed at anything, regardless of her background or previous knowledge. More recently, theorists such as Gloria Ladson-Billings have noted that a child's background and sociocultural contexts are critical in determining how to teach him. However, in Watson's time, behaviorism was a popular theory.

Edward Thorndike: Thorndike, who published in the very late 1800s and early 1900s, is a well-known educational psychologist who coined the phrase "law of effect." This law states that a response that is given a satisfactory outcome will be repeated, while a response that incurs a negative outcome will be less likely to happen again in the future. Thorndike's most famous experiment was with cats. He placed the cat in a box that had an escape lever. Whenever the cat pressed the lever, the cat was able to escape from the box. After learning this favorable consequence, the cat continued to press the lever.

B. F. Skinner: It is important to be aware of Thorndike because his work was a precursor to Skinner's work on operant conditioning. Skinner, a psychologist, theorized that behavior will be based on events that have occurred immediately prior to the action.

B. F. Skinner took this idea further when he put rats in a cage with a lever. The rats learned the lever dispensed food, and they continued to push it. In another experiment, Skinner gave a shock to the rats in a different chamber, and the rats learned quickly how not to receive shocks. This is called reinforcement—the idea that one consequence will teach an animal to repeat or not repeat a certain behavior. Additionally, avoidance behaviors are when the animal (or person) avoids a certain behavior, knowing the consequence.

This is called reinforcement—the idea that one consequence will teach an animal to repeat or not repeat a certain behavior.

STAGE NUMBER CRISIS	VIRTUE		AGE IT APPEARS
1	Trust vs. mistrust	Is the world a safe place? Bonding with caregiver: **Hope**	Birth to age 1
2	Autonomy vs. shame	Caregiver encourages independence; helps child develop self-control: **Will**	Toddler to age 3
3	Initiative vs. guilt	Imaginative play, asserting independence, curiosity; caregiver should respect child and not overprotect: **Purpose**	Preschooler, ages 3 to 5
4	Industry vs. inferiority	Academic progress, peer group influence, pride in accomplishments; parents should be encouraging: **Competence**	Grade schooler, ages 5to 12
5	Ego identity vs. role confusion	Independence, looking toward future, new sense of self: **Fidelity**	Teenager, ages 12 to 18
6	Intimacy vs. isolation	Exploring relationships, intimacy, commitment: Love	Young adult, ages 18 to 40
7	Generativity vs. stagnation	Establish career, give back to society: **Care**	Adult, ages 40 to 65
8	Ego integrity vs. despair	Explore life, remember the past, accept death without fear: **Wisdom**	Older adult, ages 65 and up

McLeod, S. A. (2007). Edward Thorndike. Retrieved from
http://www.simplypsychology.org/edward-thorndike.html

http://www.simplypsychology.org/Erik-Erikson.html
Retrieved Oct. 28, 2014.

> ## SKILL 3.2 Understands the implications of foundational motivation theories for instruction, learning, and classroom management

> ## SKILL 3.2.1 Defines terms related to foundational motivation theory, such as self-determination, attribution, extrinsic/intrinsic motivation, cognitive dissonance, classic and operant conditioning, positive and negative reinforcement

Students will not succeed without motivation. Teachers need to be aware of various theories of motivation and know how to use motivational strategies in Students will not succeed without motivation. Teachers need to be aware of various theories of motivation and know how to use motivational strategies in the classroom. While some strategies may work for one type of students, it may be necessary to use a different strategy for another type of students. Therefore, being aware of as many techniques as possible will help diversify your methods of instruction.

Self-determination: Explored by Dr. Richard Ryan and Dr. Edward Deci, self-determination theory states that, "intrinsic motivation . . . and thus higher quality learning, flourishes in contexts that satisfy human needs for competence, autonomy, and relatedness" (http://www.apa.org/research/action/success.aspx). So, what does that mean for educators? Students need to be given opportunities to explore and create, be given appropriate feedback, and be respected and heard. The theory states that when these requirements are met, students will be more engaged in the material and therefore be more successful.

Attribution: Initially developed by Fritz Heider and later discussed by Bernard Weiner, the theory of attribution argues that a person will want to understand why a certain event has happened and what she can do in the future to control the event and perhaps create different outcome. Students are influenced by their background schema and sociocultural contexts when making decisions about why an event has occurred. For example, if a child is sent out to the hallway for talking, he may believe that there were a few causes for this consequence. Perhaps another student provoked him, perhaps he was bored and therefore acted out, or perhaps he was thinking about something else and not following the rules of the classroom. Whatever he decides to be the cause will help him decide how to act in the future.

> The theory of attribution argues that a person will want to understand why a certain event has happened and what she can do in the future to control the event and perhaps create different outcome.

Extrinsic/intrinsic motivation: A child who is extrinsically motivated is only motivated by outside factors. For example, he will work for a prize, a good grade, a piece of candy, or a promised gift. He will not think about what he is learning or be metacognitive about the process. An adult who is extrinsically motivated only goes to work to collect his paycheck and does not enjoy his work or his role in his job. In contrast, a person who is intrinsically motivated is working toward an inward goal. This person is concerned about learning new material, wants to grow in his contribution to society, or feels that pushing himself to succeed for the sole reason of success is the most important goal. Most likely, he enjoys his work, and although he wouldn't mind a reward, he works for his own personal goals.

> **EXTRINSIC/INTRINSIC MOTIVATION:** A child who is extrinsically motivated is only motivated by outside factors.

> A person who is intrinsically motivated is working toward an inward goal.

Cognitive dissonance: Cognitive dissonance is a disconnect between what a child knows and what she is trying to learn. This is particularly obvious when a child learns something that doesn't make sense or fit with what she already knows. For example, if a child is convinced that a dolphin is a fish and learns that it is a mammal, reconciling this new information with what she thought she already knew will create cognitive dissonance.

> Cognitive dissonance is a disconnect between what a child knows and what she is trying to learn.

Classic and operant conditioning: These two behavioral psychology concepts, explored by Pavlov and Skinner, respectively, discuss two different processes of learning. Classic conditioning focuses on placing a signal before an involuntary behavior. Pavlov's well-known experiments with dogs explain classic conditioning. Pavlov sounded a tone before feeding dogs, and he soon noticed that the dogs began to drool just hearing the tone because they had been trained that the food would immediately follow the tone. The drooling is an automatic response; it is not under the dog's control. The tone is called the conditioned stimulus, and the drooling is called the conditioned response (http://psychology.about.com/od/behavioralpsychology/a/classical-vs-operant-conditioning.htm).

It is important to note that there are no incentives or punishments in classical conditioning, but in operant conditioning the person must make a particular decision, and because of that decision, will be rewarded or punished.

Positive and negative reinforcement: Teachers and parents use reinforcement all the time to encourage a child to act a certain way. Basically, positive reinforcement involves giving a child something, whereas negative reinforcement involves taking something away. For example, a teacher may reward good listening with stickers or extra recess time. It is important to understand that negative reinforcement is not punishment. Instead of trying to decrease a behavior, like a punishment would do, negative reinforcement is trying to increase the behavior. So, a teacher may remove something negative to increase a behavior. Perhaps her students dislike taking weekly quizzes and always act out right before the quiz. So, she removes the quiz and replaces it with an oral "review," which she grades but which creates less stress for the students.

References for this section:

http://www.apa.org/research/action/success.aspx
Retrieved Oct. 30, 2014.

http://www.learningandteaching.info/learning/dissonance.htm
Retrieved Oct. 30, 2014.

http://psychology.about.com/od/behavioralpsychology/
a/classical-vs-operant-conditioning.htm Retrieved Oct. 30, 2014.

http://nspt4kids.com/parenting/the-difference-between-positive
-and-negative-reinforcement/ Retrieved Oct. 30, 2014.

Anderman, E., and L. Anderman. "Attribution theory"
http://www.education.com/reference/article/attribution-theory/
Retrieved Oct. 30, 2014.

SKILL 3.2.2 Relates motivation theory to instruction, learning, and classroom management

Instruction: It is important to give your students an opportunity to be intrinsically motivated whenever possible. Explain why these skills are important and when they will use them in the real world. These explanations will help students

> The tone is called the conditioned stimulus, and the drooling is called the conditioned response.

> Basically, positive reinforcement involves giving a child something, whereas negative reinforcement involves taking something away.

see why they are learning the concepts and will give them an inward goal to be successful. Intrinsic motivation takes time to cultivate, and although a teacher may be managing her classroom with extrinsic motivating strategies, she needs to be teaching her students to be metacognitive as well. Self-reflections, peer assessments, and journaling can be strategies for teachers to help students become metacognitive—to learn about how they learn. Students need to understand how they learn, what they need to be successful, and why these concepts are important to their lives. Create authentic, real-world assignments that connect an abstract concept to a concrete example. When students can see why they are learning what they are learning, they are more apt to be motivated to learn to take part in society, not just to earn a prize.

Learning: In an ideal situation, students learn because they want to learn. But learning is an active process, and if students don't want to take part in it they will not succeed. Therefore, the teacher may need to resort to some extrinsic motivators to help her students understand the importance of the new material. Operant conditioning would work well in this situation. When a student performs well, is engaged in learning, and raises her hand or participates, the teacher responds with praise and enthusiasm. The other students learn that this is the behavior that the teacher wants, so they begin making these choices as well. The teacher has now taught her students that if they make certain choices (engaging in material and answering questions), they will be praised.

> When a student performs well, is engaged in learning, and raises her hand or participates, the teacher responds with praise and enthusiasm. The other students learn that this is the behavior that the teacher wants, so they begin making these choices as well.

Classroom management: Many teachers use motivating behavior management systems, such as a token economy or a behavior modification chart, to give students opportunities to earn fake money and prizes for a job well done. These systems work well in classrooms where school lessons are not in the forefront of a student's mind, in classrooms where students struggle and need more support, or in classrooms with varying levels of academic strengths. You may use positive reinforcement to reward students and take away stressors (negative reinforcements) whenever possible. Other class rewards can include extra recess, a free homework pass, or a special party for the students when they reach a particular goal, perhaps in reading, or a certain average score on an exam.

SKILL 3.3 **Knows principles and strategies for classroom management**

SKILL 3.3.1 **Knows how to develop classroom routines and procedures**

Classroom procedures and routines should begin the first day of school. For the first few weeks of school, focus on routines and procedures rather than on academic content and standards. Students should be familiar with how to do rote, common tasks that will be unique to each classroom, such as how to enter and exit the room, hand in homework, ask to use the restroom, sharpen a pencil, have a group discussion, or work in centers. Additionally, it is imperative to practice safety drills, such as fire, tornado, and intruder drills. Often, the school will have a procedure that teachers are expected to follow, but it is the teacher's responsibility to instruct students on how to act during emergency situations.

For young students, color charts with illustrations can be very helpful. For example, you may put a three-step process at your work centers. Keep the directions simple and easy to follow; for example, "take out materials," "work quietly on your task and use inside voices," and "put away materials when you are finished." Each direction can have a simple and colorful explanation. When teaching students how to use centers, give them a few minutes to spend at centers and extend the time slowly as they practice handling the responsibility. Make sure they understand how to read the directions and what the expectations are for when they are working independently.

Older students may respond to helping create the rules themselves. In the first few days, brainstorming sessions about responsibilities can help students take ownership over the class and be more motivated to follow the rules. Give students a chance to practice these rules, even if they are in middle school or high school. Some rules, such as safety procedures, are going to be extremely important and must be practiced on a regular basis. Other rules, like going to the bathroom or managing classroom discussions, can be practiced with humor so that students understand the relative importance and the gravity of different rules.

SKILL 3.3.2 Knows how to maintain accurate records

First, and most importantly, student records must be kept confidential at all times. There may be times when other school personnel, such as administrators, school therapists, or special education teachers, need to see them, and parents may request permission to access student records, but student records should not be handled lightly. While some records, such as progress testing or classroom work, will be kept in a locked file cabinet in the classroom, other more confidential records, such as state testing scores and medical records, will be kept in a locked cabinet in the school or nurse's office.

What types of records should a teacher keep? There are many instances in which a teacher will have the opportunity to record a piece of data about a student. For example, quizzes, papers, projects, and classroom work could all go into a portfolio for use at parent/teacher conferences or when looking for patterns in student work. More formal academic data, such as benchmark testing and state testing, will go in student records that will most likely be kept in the office.

Teachers will also want to keep records of parent communication. Emails, notes home, and even summaries of phone calls can all help when deciding how to handle situations by summarizing what was done in the past and how a student and the parent responded. Keeping track of parent communication can also protect the teacher. For example, if a parent accuses a teacher of not being communicative, the teacher can point to her records of communication to demonstrate that this is not true.

http://www.washington.edu/teaching/teaching-resources/ assessing-student-learning-grading/ Retrieved Oct. 29, 2014.

> ## SKILL 3.3.3 Knows how to establish standards of conduct

Appropriate conduct in a classroom includes respect, calmness, active listening, and support for peers and the instructor. In the first few weeks of school, practicing routines such as how to enter and exit the class, listen to instructions, work at centers, and act in emergencies will set the stage for understanding the basic rules of conduct in a classroom. However, teachers may need to employ particular strategies to keep behaviors positive and maintain minimal interruption in instruction. One of the following systems may be appropriate:

1. **Prompt:** Using prompts, a teacher can remind students of expectations for behaviors. These prompts can take place before each mini-lesson and throughout the day. For example, before students sit on the carpet, the teacher can remind students of carpet rules and expectations. She may do this many times in the first weeks of school, and less and less as the year progresses.

2. **Modeling:** Modeling is a subconscious strategy of altering student conduct. A teacher models good behavior by showing active listening, respect for his students, enthusiasm, and engagement. He also can point out students who are making good choices by praising them in front of the class; for example, "I love how Stephen is sitting quietly waiting for instruction." This strategy works especially well with younger students, because they can see what behavior is expected by looking at the other student, and, wanting similar praise, will often make a similar choice quickly.

3. **Behavior/incentive chart:** Various colors represent various behavior choices. All students begin the day with their name clipped to the top color of the

chart. If they make a poor choice, they are asked to move their name down one color, to the warning color. The next color may be a small consequence such as a short time-out or missing half of recess. To create a positive experience for the child, make time-out a place of reflection, not punishment. You may even choose to rename it "the Peaceful Place." Place a desk with a notebook in a corner of the room. When a student sits at the Peaceful Place, she opens the notebook to a blank page. The page has three questions on it: "What was the choice that you made?" "How are you feeling about that choice?" and "What is a better choice you could have made?" If students are too young to write their feelings, they may draw a picture and then discuss with the teacher.

The next color may be missing all of recess. The final color may be a parent call home to discuss the issue. Explain that if students stay on the top color all week, they can earn a sticker or small prize.

4. **Token System:** A token economy is a popular method of running a classroom, and it is useful from higher elementary to the lower middle school grades. Students receive a type of "token" for a specific behavior. Tokens can take the form of stickers on a chart, play money, or smiley faces that students keep in their desks or put on a chart. Behaviors can range from following directions the first time, to staying on task, to completing homework or working well with a group. When students have collected a certain number of tokens, they have the opportunity to "buy" something from the class store. While some teachers keep this simple and offer a prize from a toy chest, others create complicated economies in which students can buy every privilege in the classroom. These can range from a homework pass, to a lunch with the teacher, even to a better seat in the classroom. Children become very motivated to earn these prizes, and usually behavior improves as a result of well-managed token economy.

SKILL 3.3.4 Knows how to arrange classroom space

A classroom should be organized in a way that promotes learning, gives students an opportunity for discussion, and is visually interesting. However, this may mean different things for different grade levels. For example, desk arrangement will look different in each classroom. While a first-grade teacher may prefer desks in groups for social interactions and group work, a high school English teacher may arrange desks in a large circle to facilitate group discussion. A math teacher may put all desks in rows so students can face the board, where the teacher will be spending the majority of her time. However, be sure to leave enough physical space for students to move around and not crowd one another.

Visual stimulation is imperative as well. Colorful classroom posters, classroom rules (kept succinct), a plan for the day, and, in elementary and some middle schools, a behavior incentive chart should all be on the walls for students to see. Additionally, keep visuals at student eye level. For elementary students, that means keeping the posters and incentive charts in the lower half of the wall so students can interact with any posters that measure student progress, such as reading charts or behavior incentives.

Set up your desk so you can see the majority of students at all times. For some that means the front of the classroom, and for others that means the back. Encourage boundaries in certain areas of your classroom. For example, your things and desk area may be off limits, and computer use may be on an invitation-only basis. Additionally, setting up a small table for teacher/student conferences or small-group guided instruction can give students a place to work in small groups.

Elementary teachers may set up permanent centers, such as a small library, an art station, and a computer station. Have short directions (including a visual) posted at eye level at each of these centers. Keep materials in easy-to-identify containers so students can independently take out and return items. Teachers of older students may need to place items like hall and restroom passes or a sign-out sheet within easy reach of the students so that leaving the classroom doesn't interrupt the lesson.

SKILL 3.3.5 Recognizes ways of promoting a positive learning environment

A positive learning environment comes first from the teacher himself. Your attitude will set the tone for your classroom and for how your students perceive your class. Meet them at the door each day, wishing them good morning and giving them a task. Children who know what is expected will be more engaged in material. For example, if students know that upon entering their classroom, they take a paper from the morning work bin and work on it quietly until the teacher is ready to begin, the day will start with engaged, quiet learners, instead of loud chaos.

Next, encourage students to take part in creating the culture of the class. Help them create the rules and expectations for the room, and if a student falters, remind him privately why this rule is in place and why the class decided on it as a guideline.

Keep material engaging and authentic. Create assignments that match student interest and background and develop lessons that are student directed, collaborative, and multisensory. Engage students in conversation and praise them specifically for their effort or their product. Don't just make a cursory "great job!" comment; rather, focus on that child and give a genuine remark about her progress, such as "I love how well you are listening to your partner's ideas. Excellent active listening." When using direct instruction, which you will, lead students to the answer through Socratic questioning rather than simply telling them "no." For example, if a student tries and answers incorrectly, instead of saying "no, good try," use this moment to create a positive learning experience. Find one correct piece of the response and then direct the student toward the right answer.

Encouraging parental involvement is another tactic in creating a positive environment. Send home letters and emails and make phone calls praising students, so that when you do have to make a negative phone call, it is not your first interaction with the parent. Establish contact early and use it frequently to update parents on events, student progress, and student behavior.

Finally, a teacher must be aware of the various cultures in the classroom and create an environment that is nurturing and safe for every child. If a child feels as though his own culture is important and celebrated, he will be much more likely to share his experiences, develop friendships, and have a good attitude toward school.

> *When using direct instruction, lead students to the answer through Socratic questioning rather than simply telling them "no." For example, if a student tries and answers incorrectly, instead of saying "no, good try," use this moment to create a positive learning experience. Find one correct piece of the response and then direct the student toward the right answer.*

SKILL 3.4 Knows a variety of strategies for helping students develop self-motivation

SKILL 3.4.1 Assigning valuable tasks

Busywork such as worksheets or silent reading time may bore students, because these activities don't require active engagement. In contrast, authentic assignments that require students to seek questions and answers or that relate the content to their own life will motivate them to move forward in their work. Be available to your students throughout the process of learning and through any formative assessments. Be a facilitator, ask questions, scaffold when necessary, and always make students feel important and engaged. When you are teaching new information, use lecture and direct instruction when necessary but remember that students' attention spans may not be long, so use lecture sparingly. Instead, create opportunities for students to share their own experiences, use cooperative learning, take ownership of the work they are doing, and ask questions and have dialogue about what they are learning.

Additionally, be wary of summative assessments and homework assignments. Keep homework as brief as possible, engaging, and important. For example, it may be appropriate to assign 10 math problems to check for understanding, but it may be too much to assign 30. When giving summative assessments, try not to give them too often, keep them as brief as possible, and encourage students to be self-reflective to work on their metacognitive skills. Self-reflective journal assignments, peer review, or self-review rubrics are all tools that can help students grow in metacognition and intrinsic motivation.

Self-motivation, or intrinsic motivation, is motivation that comes from within. Students who are intrinsically motivated succeed because they have set a goal for themselves and/or because they are interested in learning about the subject. In contrast, students who are extrinsically motivated work toward a goal because of a prize or a bribe. For example, a student who works toward completing an assignment for a piece of candy, a promised "A," or a free homework pass is extrinsically motivated. A teacher needs to find tasks for students that engage and motivate. By learning about the students' likes, dislikes, literacies, ability, sociocultural contexts, and academic abilities, a teacher will be able to find tasks that not only are engaging but also match student ability. For example, a class of gifted students will thrive with a student-directed project that encourages research and choices and allows the teacher to act as a facilitator. A class with varying abilities will thrive with centers that use differentiated instruction to connect to as many types of students as possible.

> Students who are intrinsically motivated succeed because they have set a goal for themselves and/or because they are interested in learning about the subject. In contrast, students who are extrinsically motivated work toward a goal because of a prize or a bribe.

Valuable tasks will be multisensory and use Howard Gardner's multiple intelligences to match what students need. Use direct instruction when necessary, but not often. Use worksheets and desk practice when necessary, but not often. Make sure students are active, moving, engaged, talking, and assessed in various ways.

SKILL 3.4.2 Providing frequent positive feedback

Feedback is critical to student success. Students need to know that their efforts are rewarded. Feedback can come informally, through specific compliments on effort or written compliments on turned-in work. A teacher should be attentive to all types of student participation. While some students will raise their hand and want to answer any question the teacher asks, others will sit quietly but may write analytical journal entries or complete detailed homework assignments. Find ways to compliment all students. Feedback should include parents as well. Send home consistent compliments or constructive notations so parents know how to help their child. Perhaps you have the opportunity for a weekly progress report in which you may note a child's grades on the weekly assessments, her efforts, and her behavior.

Students with low self-confidence or who often feel challenged in class will need constant feedback to continue to feel motivated. Make sure to notice their efforts, their behavior, and their academic success. For a student who struggles, every good choice is a victory. Teachers often refer to this method as "catching them being good."

The purpose of written feedback should be to guide and to teach, not to degrade or edit. Do not redo a student's work for him. Instead, make constructive suggestions and encourage him to try again. Note exactly where the mistake is and direct him to the answer, give him an opportunity to find the answer, or give him the correct answer one time so he knows it for future work. Feedback should be specific, not general, even if the deliverable is strong. For example, instead of writing "Excellent work!" write "Great job with organizing your paragraphs. You especially had a well-organized and detailed introduction."

SKILL 3.4.3 Including students in instructional decisions

While you will follow standards in creating lesson plans, you also need to be very aware of student data. What are students struggling with? What challenges them? What is easy? Looking at progress testing and state data can help determine the exact standards on which you need to be focusing. Invite students to a one-on-one conference where you can discuss their strengths and challenges. Ask them what they believe to be the concepts that are difficult for them and the concepts that are easy. Create centers that focus on concepts that need work. For example, if students are struggling with counting money, create a classroom "store" where students can buy and sell items during math time.

Additionally, students should always be aware of the objective of the day, even when they are very young. Write it on the board or include a visual; for example, "Today we will practice counting quarters and dimes. This concept will help us buy items in stores and count and sort our money." Students will understand the goal and the focus of the lesson and will be more likely to participate because they know the real-world connection to the lesson.

SKILL 3.4.4 De-emphasizing grades

Grades are going to be an important part of assessment and will be necessary when you collect data for progress reports, report cards, or state testing. However, it's important, especially in the younger grades, to de-emphasize the formal assessment process and instead stress effort, engagement, and progress. Be sure that students understand that you are looking for their engagement in the material. That may include active listening, verbal communication that there is understanding, completed assignments, or completed hands-on activities. Be sure to explain that grades are not only numbers or letters that measure quantitative progress but also reflections of effort and participation.

DOMAIN II
INSTRUCTIONAL PROCESS

PERSONALIZED STUDY PLAN

KNOWN MATERIAL/ SKIP IT

PAGE	COMPETENCY AND SKILL	
45	**4.1: Understands the role of district, state, and national standards and frameworks in instructional planning**	☐
	4.1.1: Understands the theoretical basis of standards-b ased education	☐
	4.1.2: Knows resources for accessing district, state, and national standards and frameworks	☐
	4.1.3: Understands how standards and frameworks apply to instructional planning	☐
46	**4.2: Knows how to apply the basic concepts of predominant educational theories**	☐
	4.2.1: Understands the basic concepts of cognitivism, such as schema, information processing, mapping	☐
	4.2.2: Understands the basic concepts of social learning theory, such as modeling, reciprocal determinism, vicarious learning	☐
	4.2.3: Understands the basic concepts of constructivism, such as learning as experience, problem-based learning, zone of proximal development, scaffolding, inquiry/discovery learning	☐
	4.2.4: Understands the basic concepts of behaviorism, such as conditioning, intrinsic and extrinsic rewards, reinforcement, punishment	☐
	4.2.5: Knows how to apply the basic concepts of behaviorism, constructivism, social learning theory, and congnitivism to instructional contexts	☐
49	**4.3: Understands how scope and sequence affect instructional planning**	☐
	4.3.1: Defines and provides examples of scope	☐
	4.3.2: Defines and provides examples of sequence	☐
	4.3.3: Understands the relationship between scope and sequence and standards of learning	☐
	4.3.4: Understands the role of scope and sequence in curriculum planning	☐
51	**4.4: Knows how to select content to achieve lesson and unit objectives**	☐
51	**4.5: Knows how to develop observable and measurable instructional objectives in the cognitive, affective, and psychomotor domains**	☐
	4.5.1: Distinguishes among the different learning domains	☐
	4.5.2: Knows how to apply Bloom's taxonomy to the development of instructional objectives	☐
	4.5.3: Knows how to describe observable behavior	☐
	4.5.4: Knows how to describe measurable outcomes	☐
53	**4.6: Is aware of the need for and is able to identify various resources for planning enrichment and remediation**	☐

PERSONALIZED STUDY PLAN

KNOWN MATERIAL/ SKIP IT

PAGE	COMPETENCY AND SKILL	
	4.6.1: Identifies when remediation is appropriate	☐
	4.6.2: Identifies when enrichment is appropriate	☐
	4.6.3: Identifies a variety of resources for locating, adapting, or creating enrichment and remediation activities	☐
55	**4.7: Understands the role of resources and materials in supporting student learning**	☐
	4.7.1: Identifies and explains the uses of a variety of resources and materials that support student learning, such as computers, the Internet and other electronic resources, library collections (books, magazines, pamphlets, reference works), videos, DVDs, artifacts, models, manipulatives, guest speakers and community members	☐
	4.7.2: Knows how to develop lessons as part of thematic and/or interdisciplinary units	☐
	4.7.3: Understands the basic concepts of thematic instruction	☐
	4.7.4: Understands the components of thematic units, such as selecting a theme, designing integrated learning activities, selecting resources, designing assessments	☐
	4.7.5: Understands the basic concepts of interdisciplinary instruction	☐
	4.7.6: Understands the components of interdisciplinary units, such as collaborating, generating applicable topics, developing an integrative framework, planning instruction for each discipline, designing integrative assessment, recognizes their role in collaborating with instructional partners in instructional planning	☐
	4.7.7: Identifies a variety of instructional planning partners, such as special educational teachers, library media specialists, teachers of the gifted and talented, IEP team members, para educators	☐
	4.7.8: Describe the roles each partner plays in collaborative activities	☐
62	**5.1: Understands the cognitive processes associated with learning, such as critical thinking, creative thinking, questioning, inductive and deductive reasoning, problem solving, planning, memory, recall**	☐
63	**5.2: Understands the distinguishing features of different instructional models**	☐
	5.2.1: Describes a variety of instructional models, such as direct, indirect, independent, experiential, interactive	☐
64	**5.3: Knows a variety of instructional strategies associated with each instructional model**	☐
	5.3.1: Identifies instructional strategies associated with direct instruction, such as explicit teaching, drill and practice, lecture, demonstrations, guides for reading, listening, viewing	☐
	5.3.2: Identifies instructional strategies associated with indirect instruction, such as problem solving, inquiry, case studies, concept mapping, reading for meaning, cloze procedures	☐

PERSONALIZED STUDY PLAN

KNOWN MATERIAL/ SKIP IT

PAGE	COMPETENCY AND SKILL	KNOWN MATERIAL/ SKIP IT
	5.3.3: Identifies instructional strategies associated with independent instruction, such as learning contracts, research projects, learning centers, computer mediated instruction, distance learning	☐
	5.3.4: Identifies instructional strategies associated with experiential and virtual instruction, such as field trips, experiments, simulations, role play, games, observations	☐
	5.3.5: Identifies instructional strategies associated with interactive instruction, such as brainstorming, cooperative learning groups, interviews, discussions, peer practice, debates	☐
70	**5.4: Knows a variety of strategies for encouraging complex cognitive processes**	☐
	5.4.1: Identifies complex cognitive processes, such as concept learning, problem solving, metacognition, critical thinking, transfer	☐
	5.4.2: Knows instructional activities specific to the development of complex cognitive processes, such as distinguishing fact from opinion, comparing and contrasting, detecting bias, predicting, categorizing, analyzing, sequencing, summarizing, inferring, decision making, evaluating, synthesizing, generalizing	☐
74	**5.5: Knows a variety of strategies for supporting student learning**	☐
	5.5.1: Identifies and explains uses of strategies for supporting student learning, such as modeling, developing self-regulation skills, scaffolding, differentiating instruction, guided practice, coaching	☐
77	**5.6: Knows basic strategies for promoting students' development of self-regulatory skills**	☐
	5.6.1: Knows how to support students in setting goals, managing time, organizing information, monitoring progress, reflecting on outcomes, establishing a productive work environment	☐
	5.6.2: Understands the design of different group configurations for learning	☐
	5.6.3: Describes different group configurations, such as whole-class, small-group, independent learning, one-on-one, pair/share	☐
79	**5.7: Understands the use and implications of different grouping techniques and strategies**	☐
	5.7.1: Explains the uses, strengths, and limitations of a variety of grouping techniques, such as cooperative learning, collaborative learning, heterogeneous grouping, homogeneous grouping, multi-age grouping, grouping by gender	☐
80	**5.8: Knows how to select an appropriate strategy for achieving an instructional objective**	☐

PERSONALIZED STUDY PLAN

KNOWN MATERIAL/ SKIP IT

PAGE	COMPETENCY AND SKILL	
81	**5.9: Understands the concept of monitoring and adjusting instruction in response to student feedback**	☐
	5.9.1: Explains the instructional purposes of monitoring and adjusting instruction	☐
	5.9.2: Knows strategies for monitoring and adjusting instruction	☐
82	**5.10: Recognizes the purpose of reflecting upon, analyzing, and evaluating the effectiveness of instructional strategies**	☐
83	**5.11: Knows the characteristics of different types of memory and their implications for instructional planning and student learning**	☐
	5.11.1: Distinguishes among the different types of memory, such as short term and long term (*see also Skills 4.2.1 and 5.1*)	☐
	5.11.2: Considers the characteristics and effects of memory on student learning when planning instructon	☐
84	**5.12: Recognizes the role of teachable moments in instruction**	☐
	5.12.1: Defines and provides examples of a teachable moment	☐
	5.12.2: Understands the uses of the teachable moment	☐
85	**6.1: Knows the components of effective questioning**	☐
87	**6.2: Understands the uses of questioning**	☐
	6.2.1: Explains and provides different examples of different purposes of questioning, such as developing interest and motivating students, evaluating students' preparation, reviewing previous lessons, helping students set realistic expectations, engaging students in discussion, determining prior knowledge, preparing students for what is to be learned, guiding thinking, developing critical and creative thinking skills, checking for comprehension or level of understanding, summarizing information, stimulating students to pursue knowledge on their own	☐
91	**6.3: Knows strategies for supporting students in articulating their ideas**	☐
	6.3.1: Explains and provides examples of strategies for supporting students in articulating their ideas, such as verbal and non-verbal prompting, restatement, reflective listening statements, wait time	☐
92	**6.4: Knows methods for encouraging higher levels of thinking**	☐
	6.4.1: Explains and provides examples of methods for encouraging students' higher levels of thinking, thereby guiding students to reflect, challenge assumptions, find relationships, determine relevancy and validity of information, design alternative solutions, draw conclusions, transfer knowledge	☐

PERSONALIZED STUDY PLAN

X **KNOWN MATERIAL/ SKIP IT**

PAGE	COMPETENCY AND SKILL	
92	**6.5: Knows strategies for promoting a safe and open forum for discussion**	☐
	6.5.1: Knows basic techniques for establishing and maintaining standards of conduct for discussions, such as engaging all learners, creating a collaborative environment, respecting diverse opinions, supporting risk taking	☐
94	**7.1: Understands various verbal and nonverbal communication modes**	☐
	7.1.1: Explains and provides examples of body language; gesture; tone, stress, and inflection; eye contact; facial expression; personal space	☐
95	**7.2: Is aware of how culture and gender can affect communication**	☐
96	**7.3: Knows how to use various communication tools to enrich the learning environment**	☐
	7.3.1: Audio and visual aids	☐
	7.3.2: Text and digital resources	☐
	7.3.3: Internet and other computer-based tools	☐
99	**7.4: Understands effective listening strategies**	☐
	7.4.1: Explains and provides examples of active listening strategies, such as attending to the speaker, restating key points, asking questions, interpreting information, providing supportive feedback, and being respectful	☐

COMPETENCY 4
PLANNING INSTRUCTION

SKILL 4.1 Understands the role of district, state, and national standards and frameworks in instructional planning

Teachers are not alone in their classrooms. They do not have complete freedom to teach what they want, when they want, or sometimes even how they want. There are standards, assessments, and frameworks to which they must adhere and that they must consult in conducting instructional planning.

SKILL 4.1.1 Understands the theoretical basis of standards-based education

What is standards-based education? The idea behind having national standards is that each child receives an equal education, regardless of the background of the school, the funding, or the experiences of the teacher. Each child will be taught similar concepts as he goes through school, and upon graduation, he should be on equal footing with another student who graduated from a different school. Unfortunately, this is rarely the reality, since limited resources and students' needs can get in the way of nationalized pacing. However, when No Child Left Behind was passed in 2001, schools began to look at national standards as a framework, a goal, and a basis for planning lessons. To make sure teachers are following through, statewide standardized tests given to determine how students measure on these nationalized standards are now part of the yearly curriculum.

SKILL 4.1.2 Knows resources for accessing district, state, and national standards and frameworks

The Department of Education for each state will have websites that list all national and state standards for each grade, which will usually be available as a PDF file to read and print. Teachers should keep a copy of these standards at school and at home so they are ready to match each lesson with a particular standardized objective.

District objectives are more selective and may be a combination of state and national standards, along with a few extra standards determined by district administration. Often, these resources are available in the office for new teachers as they begin planning. Additionally, if a new teacher is given a mentor, often the mentor will attend the first meeting with a copy of these standards.

SKILL 4.1.3 Understands how standards and frameworks apply to instructional planning

A teacher must begin his instructional planning with the standards he needs to cover. These state and district frameworks will give him the scope and sequence of his year. Although he may have a choice as to how to fill the instructional time, he does not have the freedom to choose what topics to teach. State tests are based on state standards, and for students to have as equal an education as possible, all students must learn comparable subject matter each year. Often, a team of teachers will meet prior to the start of the school year to discuss any content issues, student challenges, or how they will handle teaching all of the state standards in such a short amount of time. Previous test data will also guide the teachers in providing the skills that are already easy for many students and the ones that need to be consistently reviewed.

SKILL 4.2 Knows how to apply the basic concepts of predominant educational theories

It is one thing to understand the concepts behind the theory, but without knowing how to apply these concepts, an educator may miss their purpose.

SKILL 4.2.1 Understands the basic concepts of cognitivism such as schema, information processing, mapping

Cognitive learning is based on the fact that learning comes from background schema. When a child's schema has changed, or grown, the child has learned. Learning is an active process. A child takes in new information and processes it with her familiar information, eventually forming a new concept or more advanced understanding. Terms used in cognitive learning include schema, information processing, and mapping.

Schema: Schema is another word for background knowledge or prior knowledge. Teachers use prior knowledge all the time when beginning a unit; they often start by asking students what they already know. By engaging in this activity, students' prior knowledge is activated, and they can use this prior knowledge (schema) to connect to new knowledge. For example, a child may already understand that letters make sounds. When a teacher introduces blending sounds into words, she can note that the sounds now connect to make words! Students who already understand that letters connect to individual sounds will make this connection to words more quickly. Often, when teachers activate prior knowledge, they invite students to make one of three connections: text to self, text to world, or text to text. One of these connections will make the most sense to the concept taught and make an abstract concept more concrete.

Information processing: Information processing is the concept that building new knowledge depends on the type of memory working at a particular time. There are three types of memory: sensory memory, working memory, and long-term memory. Sensory memory is the fastest, but it is limited. We need sensory memory to separate relevant from irrelevant information. When new information comes in, children process it quickly. What does a student need to take in and keep, and what can she move past without committing it to her schema? If a student chooses to hold onto new information, it is moved toward the working memory, where it is committed to background schema and then put into "files" from which she can retrieve it when needed.

Long-term memory is the most permanent type of memory. Information that is stored here is automatic and important for a person to remember. Some examples of information in long-term memory are phone numbers, addresses, reading, basic math, and riding a bike.

Mapping: Mapping is a way to visualize information for easier recall. Often, people do this subconsciously, but it can also be taught in a classroom to show students how to retrieve information conceptually. When someone commits something to his long-term memory, often he uses mapping to be able to retrieve it quickly.

Shraw, G., and M. McCrudden. (2013). Information processing theory. http://www.education.com/reference/article/information -processing-theory/ Retrieved Jan. 25, 2014.

> **SKILL 4.2.2** **Understands the basic concepts of social learning theory, such as modeling, reciprocal determinism, vicarious learning**

Social learning theory, first outlined by Albert Bandura, states that learning is social and that children learn from one another, without needing any extrinsic motivators. For example, when a younger child copies the behavior of an older one, she is demonstrating the ideas of social learning theory. She watches another child and then repeats the behavior. Basic ideas of social learning theory include modeling, reciprocal determinism, and vicarious learning.

Modeling: A child learns through observations and decides if an observed behavior should be copied. A child may not change his own behavior, but he will observe another child's behavior to learn appropriate choices.

INFORMATION PROCESSING: Information processing is the concept that building new knowledge depends on the type of memory working at a particular time.

LONG-TERM MEMORY: The most permanent type of memory.

MAPPING: Mapping is a way to visualize information for easier recall.

MODELING: A child learns through observations and decides if an observed behavior should be copied. A child may not change his own behavior, but he will observe another child's behavior to learn appropriate choices.

RECIPROCAL DETERMINISM: A person will change her behavior based on reactions from others and reactions from what she sees in the environment.

Reciprocal determinism: A person will change her behavior based on reactions from others and reactions from what she sees in the environment. Children are not passive observers; rather, they decide which behaviors to change based on multiple types of interactions.

Vicarious learning: A child sees a type of behavior and chooses to replicate it based on the consequences of the behavior. For example, if a child is following directions well and the teacher compliments that child, other children take note and also begin to follow directions well.

> **VICARIOUS LEARNING:** A child sees a type of behavior and chooses to replicate it based on the consequences of the behavior.

SKILL 4.2.3 **Understands the basic concepts of constructivism, such as learning as experience, problem-based learning, zone of proximal development, scaffolding, inquiry/discovery learning**

A teacher in a constructivist classroom is a facilitator, not a direct instructor. This philosophy is based on writings from theorists such as Bruner and Vygotsky. In these environments, the teacher does not lecture. Instead, he facilitates student learning through problem solving and problem-based learning. Concepts included in the constructivist classroom include problem-based learning, zone of proximal development, scaffolding, and inquiry/discovery learning.

Problem-based learning and inquiry/discovery learning: These student-centered approaches are critical to a constructivist classroom. In a problem-based learning situation, the teacher poses a problem to small groups, and the students research and find solutions. Often, these problems are authentic to the students' lives, and they always are engaging. In inquiry/discovery learning, the students choose their own subject for research and develop a path to solving the problem.

Zone of proximal development/scaffolding: These terms, developed by Vygotsky, refer to a child's independence level. The ZPD (zone of proximal development) is the area between what a child can do on her own and what a child can do with a teacher's assistance. Often, a teacher will help, or scaffold, students through the ZPD so they can develop independence in a new area of understanding. This process can take time and can be frustrating, but is an important piece of developing a child's conceptual understanding.

SKILL 4.2.4 **Understands the basic concepts of behaviorism, such as conditioning, intrinsic and extrinsic rewards, reinforcement, punishment**

Initially discussed by educational theorists such as Pavlov, Watson, and Skinner, the behaviorism focus on the idea that behavior can be changed by altering the environment and the stimulus surrounding a positive or negative action. Concepts include conditioning, intrinsic versus extrinsic rewards, reinforcement, and punishment.

Conditioning: Conditioning refers to a change in behavior based on changes in the environment. Two main types of conditioning, operant and classical, are the main tenets of behaviorism. Operant conditioning refers to modifying voluntary behaviors, while classical conditioning involves involuntary behaviors.

Intrinsic versus extrinsic rewards: An intrinsic reward is an inner motivation. A person succeeds at a skill because she feels it is important, and she does not need any external stimulus. Alternatively, a person who works for extrinsic rewards needs an outside prize to feel that her actions are worthwhile. Extrinsic rewards can include money or a promotion, or, for a child, a sticker or treat.

Reinforcement/punishment: These are the backbone of operant conditioning. Reinforcement is when a person receives something (often after making a good choice), and punishment refers to having something taken away (often after making a bad choice).

SKILL 4.2.5 Knows how to apply the basic concepts of behaviorism, constructivism, social learning theory, and cognitivism to instructional contexts

Teachers will have an opportunity to focus on each of these concepts in their classrooms. No teacher will focus on one all the time. For example, when a teacher is trying to alter student behavior, he will most likely use a combination of behaviorism (reinforcement/punishment, rewards) and social learning theory (discussing the needs of the classroom and how all students can help the group succeed). A teacher may also use social learning theory when he discusses new academic concepts: Why are we learning these concepts? How will this knowledge make us better citizens? Students will respond to new concepts when they know the purpose behind their learning. When a teacher is beginning a new concept, he will most likely turn to constructivist ideas, scaffolding his students heavily as they first learn and then pushing them through their zone of proximal development to the next level.

SKILL 4.3 Understands how scope and sequence affect instructional planning

SKILL 4.3.1 Defines and provides examples of scope

Scope is another word for what an educator is teaching. What concepts will be the focus of the unit? What should students have mastered by

---

CONDITIONING: Conditioning refers to a change in behavior based on changes in the environment. Two main types of conditioning, operant and classical, are the main tenets of behaviorism.

INTRINSIC VERSUS EXTRINSIC REWARDS: An intrinsic reward is an inner motivation. A person succeeds at a skill because she feels it is important, and she does not need any external stimulus. Alternatively, a person who works for extrinsic rewards needs an outside prize to feel that her actions are worthwhile. Two main types of conditioning, operant and classical, are the main tenets of behaviorism.

REINFORCEMENT/ PUNISHMENT: These are the backbone of operant conditioning. Reinforcement is when a person receives something (often after making a good choice), and punishment refers to having something taken away (often after making a bad choice).

the end of the unit? For example, after a fifth grader completes a unit on the Revolutionary War, he may have learned the main causes of the war, the major challenges faced by both sides, a few of the leaders, and the way the conflict was resolved. This content would have been objectives provided by the teacher at the start of the unit. Skills in this unit may have included finding main idea, inference, research skills, fact versus opinion, and completing graphic organizers that discuss cause and effect. Scope almost always covers the mandated district and state standards, although it is up to the teacher to choose exactly when and how to implement them.

SKILL 4.3.2 — Defines and provides examples of sequence

Sequence is another word for order. In what order will the content be taught? Which skills will come first, and which will come last? Sometimes, the district will make these decisions, but often, lead or team teachers can choose the sequence of material at the start of the school year. Often, the choice is based on students' prior knowledge, when state testing occurs, and natural order. For example, a course on American history will most likely go in chronological order, so students can use what they have learned about prior historical events to understand more current ones.

SKILL 4.3.3 — Understands the relationship between scope and sequence and standards of learning

SKILL 4.3.4 — Understands the role of scope and sequence in curriculum planning

Scope is what a student learns, and sequence is the order in which she learns it. These two concepts are connected, and because standards of learning are the backbone of teacher lesson planning, there is a strong relationship between all three. Teachers base their instruction on standards of learning, which detail the skills that students must learn in a calendar year. Often, standards of learning are created in terms of a specific sequence. For example, an educator may see the main idea in advance of inference skills. A student needs to understand how to find the main idea before he is able to infer ideas from the text. So, a teacher often can move through the standards sequentially, knowing that skills build upon one another. Occasionally, it may be wise to skip a certain set of standards and come back to it later, but only if student understanding and prior knowledge makes this the most efficient strategy.

When a teacher is planning her curriculum, she will evaluate the scope of what she has to teach, the time she has to teach it, what her students already understand, and what they need to know. This will guide her in planning how long units will be, what each day will look like, what her formative and summative assessments will be, and how she will sequence her unit.

SKILL 4.4 Knows how to select content to achieve lesson and unit objectives

How do you know if your content is going to achieve the lesson and the unit objectives? First, plan according to scope and sequence. What are the goals of the unit? What skills should students master? Additionally, what are the content and skill goals for the unit? District and state standards may set the bar for academic objectives, but the teacher may have some freedom in choosing the type of lessons and assessments.

Choose lessons that will be multisensory and will appeal to the entire student population. Keep your classroom culturally responsive, as noted by Gloria Ladson-Billings. Students need to be engaged in the material and also must feel that the lessons are authentic and relevant to their lives. Alternate teaching methods, using direct instruction, collaborative work, and independent work. Use outside resources when available, such as community speakers, other teachers at the school, and technology, to give students extra opportunities for understanding. Additionally, keep in mind student skill level. Understand student proficiency in each content area (writing, reading, comprehending) and include activities that match these levels. Be sure to include some enrichment and remediation activities so that all students have a chance to understand and master the material.

Connect all lessons by focusing on one theme or unit goal and objective. Remind students of the goals each day prior to beginning the lesson. Explain why this content is important and how it affects their lives. Assess students often, through informal and formal opportunities. Check for understanding and repeat lessons when necessary, if time permits.

SKILL 4.5 Knows how to develop observable and measurable instructional objectives in the cognitive, affective, and psychomotor domains

SKILL 4.5.1 Distinguishes among the different learning domains

There are four major learning domains: cognitive, affective, psychomotor, and interpersonal. Before planning any lessons, a teacher needs to know which learning domain will be the focus so that he can create lessons that prioritize the concept within that particular framework.

COGNITIVE DOMAIN: This framework is familiar to educators because it is the most common classroom learning domain.

AFFECTIVE DOMAIN: This domain has to do with participation, motivation, and willingness to learn.

PSYCHOMOTOR DOMAIN: This domain is focused on motor skills and how well a student can perform a sequence of kinesthetic activities.

INTERPERSONAL DOMAIN: This domain is about interaction—students working together.

Cognitive domain: This framework is familiar to educators because it is the most common classroom learning domain. A student goes from basic to more advanced skills as understanding increases. Bloom's taxonomy is an excellent representation of how cognition in a concept improves as a student becomes familiar with the ideas.

Affective domain: This domain has to do with participation, motivation, and willingness to learn. How ready are students to learn? How motivated are they to move past challenges? Are they participating willingly? Instructors can create motivating factors through engaging and authentic material and by using collaborative activities to make learning fun. Without motivation, there will be very little cognitive change, so this domain is important to student success.

Psychomotor domain: This domain is focused on motor skills and how well a student can perform a sequence of kinesthetic activities. Common examples of psychomotor domain skills are coordination, lab work, or even participating in theater or music performance.

Interpersonal domain: This domain is about interaction—students working together. Conversation problem solving can include activities such as compromising, summarizing, disagreeing, finding solutions, and building an answer collaboratively. Often, students learn interpersonal skills from practice, guided collaborative learning, and peer and self-feedback.

Vinson, C. Learning domains and delivery of instruction. http://pixel.fhda.edu/id/learning_domain.html Retrieved Jan. 26, 2015.

SKILL 4.5.2 **Knows how to apply Bloom's taxonomy to the development of instructional objectives**

Bloom's taxonomy measures the type of understanding a student has about a concept. When a student first learns about a topic, she will have very basic understanding and may only be able to recall simple facts, which puts her into the lowest part of the pyramid. However, as her understanding increases, she will be able to analyze, synthesize, and evaluate these concepts, all of which are higher levels of Bloom's taxonomy. So, how can a teacher apply these principles to her instructional objectives? She can apply them by beginning slowly and encouraging mastery learning before moving toward new levels of understanding. For example, she may encourage students to learn their multiplication facts (which require rote memorization) before moving on to long division, which is a more conceptual idea. Additionally, as students become more advanced in their understanding, assessments will become more analytical. A first assessment may be basic recall, but later, students can solve problems, evaluate issues, and synthesize solutions.

SKILL 4.5.3 Knows how to describe observable behavior

To be measurable, a behavior must be observable and quantifiable. Behaviors that a teacher can observe, record, and count are quantifiable. How often did Timothy get off task? How often did Javier speak to his neighbor instead of raise his hand? These are not subjective behaviors. Subjective behaviors may include a child's motivation level, his interest, or any inferences the teacher may have. Those are not observable; they are qualitative. A teacher who is looking to observe needs to find behaviors he can count and then use to look for patterns in student success or failure. For example, Maria brought in her homework correctly done 10 days in a row and then received an A on the assessment. This shows that completing her homework helped her succeed on the exam. Or, during class today, Javier spent 10 minutes out of his seat sharpening his pencil, visiting the bathroom, and wandering around the room. These are off-task behaviors. It is impossible to say whether Javier enjoyed the lesson. He may have, but this is a subjective guess and not an observable behavior.

SKILL 4.5.4 Knows how to describe measurable outcomes

Teachers must use specific words when writing lesson plans to make objectives measurable. Again, the objectives must be quantifiable. Objectives such as "students will be able to describe, evaluate, create, synthesize . . ." are measurable through assessments. In each unit, a teacher is going to measure two items: knowledge and skill. What knowledge did the child gain? And what new skills has he obtained? For example, after first graders spend a week on rhyming words, the goals may be: "Students will define what 'rhyme' means. Students will be able to identify pairs of rhyming words. Students will be able to create sets of one-syllable rhyming words. Students will be able to evaluate if a word rhymes with another when there are three extra words in the list that do not rhyme."

In this example, students are learning about the definition of rhyme and will be able to identify rhyme (knowledge). Additionally, the teacher is moving up Bloom's taxonomy by teaching students how to create their own rhyme and identify rhyme where there are extraneous words (skills).

SKILL 4.6 Is aware of the need for and is able to identify various resources for planning enrichment and remediation

Enrichment and remediation are important pieces of lesson planning, because all students will not be on the same level. Teachers need to be aware of when these extra parts of their lesson are important and how to find resources for both.

SKILL 4.6.1 Identifies when remediation is appropriate

Remediation is defined as extra academic preparation in particular subjects. A student may struggle in reading, writing, math, or even organization or conceptual understanding. Sometimes, identification of remediation is easy, for example, when a child has an IEP, in which his needs are clearly stated and his team of teachers can work together to provide remediation. However, sometimes it is unclear if a child needs extra help. Perhaps a child has received a few poor grades, isn't participating in class, and has not been succeeding in his classwork. The teacher may elect to give him some extra attention, whether in the form of a tutoring class, a peer tutoring opportunity, or a few minutes of focused attention during class.

SKILL 4.6.2 Identifies when enrichment is appropriate

Enrichment is the opposite of remediation. Enrichment is more challenging work, often given to gifted and talented students or to students who are obviously exceeding the expectations for a particular piece of content. Again, sometimes identifying who needs enrichment is easy. The child is identified through test scores or through acceptance into a gifted and talented program. However, sometimes it is unclear when a child needs enrichment activities. Perhaps the student is finishing his work quickly, and his answers are correct. Perhaps he is not always correct, but he is really enjoying the topic being studied, and giving him enrichment work would be a fantastic opportunity to extend his knowledge of a topic about which he is already passionate. Enrichment can come in the form of partner work, outside projects, research time in the library or online, an extra presentation, or another authentic assignment. The goal of enrichment work is to find an assignment that is engaging and authentic—an assignment that is meaningful to the child's life. Seatwork and homework are not useful enrichment activities. The goal is to create more interest, not drown a child in busywork.

SKILL 4.6.3 Identifies a variety of resources for locating, adapting, or creating enrichment and remediation activities

Where do you look for remediation or enrichment activities? Often, an educator will find some ideas at the end of each section or chapter of a textbook. Additionally, it is always useful to ask various team members, such as special education teachers, gifted and talented teachers, or even teachers who teach the grade below or above yours, for activities. Certain websites, such as readwritethink.org, are also excellent resources for various multisensory activities for skills and concepts. When creating new lessons, remember that enrichment and remediation activities should be both multisensory and engaging. Work from student interests and backgrounds to create an authentic conceptual exercise that will both challenge and be meaningful to your students. Often, the Internet can be useful as a springboard for such activities, but it's important to adapt them to your student base.

> **SKILL 4.7** **Understands the role of resources and materials in supporting student learning**

Many teachers have multiple resources in their school for use in the classroom. However, some teachers do not take advantage of these resources and instead continue to rely on the traditional textbooks offered by the district. It's important to know what is available and to use as many resources as possible to develop high student engagement.

> **SKILL 4.7.1** **Identifies and explains the uses of a variety of resources and materials that support student learning, such as computers, the Internet and other electronic resources, library collection (books, magazines, pamphlets, reference works), videos, DVDs, artifacts, models, manipulatives, guest speakers and community members**

Computers/Internet/electronic resources: Students are constantly online. Although they spend a good amount of time on social media sites, they may not understand the academic uses of the Internet. There are many resource sites, but some are useless or not reputable. When teaching students how to research online, it's critical to explain that anyone can put anything online, and therefore, discerning between credible and noncredible websites is critical. Additionally, teaching Internet safety is paramount. Give students scavenger hunts or short research projects, giving them a list of sites to visit to find the answers. As they become more comfortable researching online, they may be able to find their own websites for answers.

Library collections: The library is stocked with books, magazines, internet and technological resources, and referenceworks, waiting for students who are learning how to conduct well-rounded research. Instead of just using the Internet, require students to visit the library and use two to three hard-copy sources for a project. Although much information can be found online, it is important that students are able to look through and find useful material in books or reference materials. Often, the librarian will run short classes for students on basic reference skills and can help students locate useful resources.

Videos/DVDs: If used sparingly, videos and DVDs can bring an aspect of a unit to life in a way that a textbook cannot. For example, a teacher may show a video that explores a math concept, and students will identify more with the cartoon on the video that on the homework worksheet. The teacher may also use videos to help historical contexts come alive. It is important to keep student engagement high during a video, so often teachers provide students with scavenger hunts to complete as the video plays. This may not be the best tactic, however, since students may focus on hearing the answers and miss the gestalt of the video. An alternative would be to ask general comprehension questions after the video is completed and help students discuss the purpose of the video and how it furthered their understanding.

Artifacts/models: Artifacts from specific time periods or items that students can touch can be very useful to their conceptual understanding. Models can be built by the teacher or by the students. Often, a fantastic summative assessment is to ask students, in collaborative groups, to build a model of what they have studied. Students can work together to research the model and can build it using parts in the classroom or brought from home. It's important not to require students to purchase materials for projects like these. Some families cannot afford these extraneous materials, so teachers should either provide materials or give students options for obtaining them.

Manipulatives: Manipulatives are critical hands-on learning tools for students in all grade levels, but they are especially useful in elementary schools. For example, when teaching students how to identify various coins, an instructor may place various play money samples at a center. When students reach this center, they can play BINGO or matching games or create patterns with these manipulatives. Later, students can work on an independent center where they play "store" with the coin manipulatives.

Guest speakers and community speakers: Guest speakers and community speakers can be an excellent way to make a unit come alive for students. For example, a first-grade class that is studying "our community" can have a visit from a firefighter, police officer, or EMT. These community members can talk about their job and what they do for the community. Speaking to community members in a relaxed atmosphere can help students conceptualize their town in a concrete way. Students have an opportunity to listen, see the uniform and accessories, ask questions, and interact with important community members.

SKILL 4.7.2 Knows how to develop lessons as part of thematic and/or interdisciplinary units

The idea behind creating a thematic unit is to help students envision the big picture so they do not see new concepts in a vacuum. When creating thematic or interdisciplinary units, keep reminding students of the purpose, goals, and objectives of the unit. Use similar vocabulary as lessons continue so students internalize conceptual words. Relate as many subjects as possible so students see the social and cognitive context behind the unit. Keep lessons focused and moving toward a goal and objective, and keep assessments multisensory and formative as well as summative.

SKILL 4.7.3 Understands the basic concepts of thematic instruction

What is thematic instruction? Basically, it is organizing a group of lessons around a particular theme, idea, or concept. In elementary school, for example, a teacher may begin a unit on underwater sea life. While he is teaching his students about the various creatures that live in the ocean, he will create lessons for each subject that center on sea life. Students will read books about sea life, make graphs that identify types of classifications, create maps, and participate in centers that are focused on sea life. Often, a theme will last three to four weeks and will cover as many aspects of sea life as are developmentally appropriate and also cover various standards of learning in many subjects. A teacher will create sea life lessons in language arts, math, science, and social studies. When a student sees a theme across her entire day, she will make stronger and more meaningful connections and will have more opportunities to master her understanding. Thematic units are also excellent for English language learners, because the natural repetition gives these students an opportunity to make sense of the concept without feeling overwhelmed with many different and unrelated subjects.

SKILL 4.7.4 Understands the components of thematic units such as selecting a theme, designing integrated learning activities, selecting resources, designing assessments

Because a thematic unit is often extensive, it includes many components. Often, teachers spend weeks preparing units before beginning instruction. So, what does a teacher need to know when designing a thematic unit? First, the teacher must determine the audience for and objectives of the unit. What is the age of the audience, what is their prior knowledge (the instructor may have to make an educated guess about this based on prior test scores and student participation), and what types of activities do these students respond to well? Additionally, the standards of learning may dictate the scope and sequence of the unit.

Next, the teacher will create learning activities that integrate multiple subject areas; cover the scope of the unit; and are multisensory, multileveled, and engaging. Examples include some direct instruction, collaborative activities, computer activities, hands-on centers, formative and summative assessments, and reflection. The lessons will cover language arts, math, science, and social studies and integrate all standards, but they will stay within the unit of learning. The instructor will select texts that match the theme and will design assessments that integrate all subjects covered. Assessments can include exams, but they should also include more hands-on projects such as interviews, presentations, journals, and participation logs.

On the first day of the thematic unit, the instructor will explain the objectives of the unit and the types of activities in which students will participate. An elementary teacher especially should be continuously explaining the connections between subjects and the theme, so that students can develop deeper understanding.

SKILL 4.7.5 Understands the basic concepts of interdisciplinary instruction

When multiple teachers of various subjects work together to create a thematic unit that stretches across disciplines, that is interdisciplinary instruction. For example, if the fifth-grade teachers are beginning a unit on the Middle Ages, perhaps the social studies, science, language arts, music, and art teachers are involved in lesson planning. For example, in language arts class, students read and analyze poetry from the Middle Ages, and in social studies, they learn about the historical context and major events that took place. The science teacher explores the medical challenges during the Middle Ages and what was learned from the diseases that took so many lives. In music, students study the type of instruments played during the Middle Ages, and in art, the students may replicate some famous pieces.

Why use interdisciplinary instruction? First and foremost, it gives students a much more in-depth understanding of the theme. Instead of learning about a concept from one teacher, students have the opportunity to learn about the many facets of a time period or concept from varying points of views. What interests one student may not interest another, but with so many opportunities to learn, students have multiple chances to engage with and understand the material. Because there is such a strong connection across disciplines, there is less confusion for the students. During the unit, they know exactly what they will be studying in each class and can use knowledge from one discipline to help understand another.

SKILL Understands the components of interdisciplinary units such as
4.7.6 collaborating, generating applicable topics, developing an integrative framework, planning instruction for each discipline, designing integrative assessment, recognizes their role in collaborating with instructional partners in instructional planning

When creating an interdisciplinary unit, an educator must keep in mind the components. Although planning interdisciplinary units is similar to planning regular thematic units, there are some important differences.

Collaborating: Interdisciplinary instruction includes teamwork. Multiple teachers will be working together to carry a theme across disciplines. For example, the social studies, science, language arts, and music teacher may collaborate in creating a unit that not only fits all the standards for each subject area but also connects to the theme.

Generating applicable topics: Applicable topics must connect to all subject areas. For example, the language arts teacher needs to teach a novel, and the social studies teacher needs to teach about the Revolutionary War. Why not combine the two? The social studies teacher can give the history of the subject, and the language arts teacher can choose an appropriate novel for the theme. This way, the students learn that this subject is not just something they work on in social studies, but it has implications across other disciplines.

Developing an integrative framework/planning instruction for each discipline/designing integrative assessment: Team teachers will develop a scope and sequence based on district and state standards that covers all needed material and engages students in multisensory lessons. Lessons must be clear, concise, and focused. Each day in each class must have a purpose and objective, all leading toward the same goal.

When creating assessments, keep all skills and knowledge in mind. For example, it is okay for the social studies teacher to ask a question about the novel read in language arts during the interdisciplinary unit. This type of connecting question will show students again that all subject matter is connected. If there are traditional exams, follow those up with a collaborative project to give students a chance to synthesize all the information on their own. Perhaps create a presentation that can be given in front of all teachers involved, so students can receive feedback from varying points of view.

Recognizes the role in collaborating with instructional partners in instructional planning: It's important for each teacher to feel engaged in planning, teaching, and assessing. Some teachers may feel protective of their subject area and may not want to share time or even ideas about lesson planning. The first step in a successful interdisciplinary unit is teamwork, so team leaders or administrators may have to help certain educators understand the reasoning behind these units. A smooth integrative unit will keep students interest, because instead of having isolated subjects, each class will meld into the next, and there will be smooth transitions and planned connections across the disciplines.

> **SKILL 4.7.7** Identifies a variety of instructional planning partners, such as special education teachers, library media specialists, teachers of the gifted and talented, IEP team members, para educators

If you are lucky, you will have support staff within your school who have specialized talents and who can help your students succeed. Many of these staff have special training in dealing with specific types of populations and can be useful in small-group or specified instruction or with specific populations of students.

Special education teachers: Special education teachers are highly trained in the laws of special education, how to attend and chair an IEP meeting, and how to write and carry out an IEP. They are also well versed in alternative state assessments and how to manage those correctly without making mistakes. They also usually have a specialty population for which they have extra training, such as students with reading difficulties or students on the autism spectrum. Special education teachers may work in a regular education classroom as a co-teacher or in a small classroom with pull-out students. They can work well with small groups of students on specific skills, such as phonemic awareness or math concepts.

Library media specialists: These trained support staff members often work in the school library. They may teach small multimedia classes in which students learn to use the library or online search engines for research purposes. Media specialists may also run events such as school-wide book fairs or read-a-thons. They are also available to help students check out books, learn about new books, teach students how to use the Internet for research purposes, or help with a research project.

Teachers of gifted and talented students: GATE teachers are also highly trained in the unique needs of a child who has been identified as gifted. These children have specific needs based on their intense personalities and extreme talents in certain areas. These teachers know how to keep these students engaged and balance their academic needs with their distinctive social needs. GATE teachers are also prepared to work with parents at meetings and determine appropriate plans for these types of students.

Para educators: Para educators are often instructional assistants. They may or may not have a college degree, depending on the requirements of the district. Para educators may have gone through some specialized training, based on which types of students they are helping. For example, a para educator who works with overly aggressive children may have had training on how to handle physical violence in a child. Some para educators aid only one or two high-needs children, and others aid the teacher with a big or very diverse class. Be aware of your para educator's skills and give her tasks that highlight those skills. Remember that there are highly trained staff who can work with students in small groups on specific academic skills, which may be an uncomfortable task for a para educator who doesn't have the background in that particular subject area. It is always important to put the most qualified teacher with the neediest student. For example, a specialized teacher will be able to teach and help a student who struggles with dyslexia, whereas a para educator who hasn't had much training may be better off with a less stressful task.

SKILL 4.7.8 Describe the roles each partner plays in collaborative activities

Each of these professionals will play a different role in collaborative activities, depending on the goal of the activity. A teacher should use all of these resources whenever he feels it necessary; these professionals are there to support the students and give teachers additional help. For instance, para educators are helpful on a daily basis; most are in the classroom with the teacher. A para educator can work with small groups, help manage student behavior, or even prepare lessons for the next day. Other more specialized staff, such as special education teachers, therapists, or gifted and talented teachers, can be helpful for specific students, giving general education teachers individualized work that will aid in students' understanding or challenge students. Additionally, these teachers can be useful in planning, because they will see the lessons from varied perspectives and can offer the teacher a new point of view in creating lessons and assessments.

COMPETENCY 5
INSTRUCTIONAL STRATEGIES

SKILL 5.1 Understands the cognitive processes associated with learning such as critical thinking, creative thinking, questioning, inductive and deductive reasoning, problem solving, planning, memory, recall

CRITICAL THINKING: Involves evaluating, synthesizing, comparing, contrasting, and inferring.

CREATIVE THINKING: Creative thinking is when students use their knowledge to develop new solutions to problems or to create new ideas based on background schema.

INDUCTIVE REASONING: Inductive reasoning is when a person moves from specific information to general information.

Critical thinking: Critical thinking involves evaluating, synthesizing, comparing, contrasting, and inferring. Students take evidence and arguments and move beyond recall and basic understanding into the higher levels of Bloom's taxonomy.

Creative thinking: Creative thinking is when students use their knowledge to develop new solutions to problems or to create new ideas based on background schema.

Questioning: A teacher will use questioning to help her students reach the correct answer. Often, she will use Socratic questioning, in which she guides students toward the correct thought process without ever telling them that they are incorrect. For example, if a student reaches an incorrect answer in math, the teacher may say, "Can you explain how you came to that answer?" In moving through the steps she took to reach the answer, the students may realize her mistake and be able to self-correct.

Inductive and deductive reasoning: Inductive reasoning is when a person moves from specific information to general information. For example, if a teacher wants to understand why a student is not succeeding in class, the teacher may begin by observing the student's behavior. Then the teacher will look at the student's grades, peer relationships, and home life and will eventually develop a general idea of why the student is not doing well. Deductive reasoning is when a person moves from general information to specific information. The challenge of deductive reasoning is that the initial general statement has to be correct, which is not always true. If the initial statement is false, the entire thought process will be flawed.

Problem solving: Often, teachers use problem solving in learning, because it is student-centered and engaging. When students are given a problem and asked to research a solution, working collaboratively and looking through multiple viewpoints, they are actively engaging in problem solving.

Planning: A teacher must incorporate appropriate planning in his lessons so that students feel organized and understand the goals and objectives of the scope and sequence. When a teacher has chosen goals for daily lessons and for overall units, his students will learn more and feel more successful and involved. Additionally, teachers must plan lessons and assessments to complete the goals set forth by the district and state prior to the yearly state examinations.

Memory: There are three types of memory: sensory, short term, and long term. All three are covered more extensively in this study guide (see Skill 4.2.1). Briefly, sensory memory is the fastest, but it is limited. We need sensory memory to separate relevant from irrelevant information. Short-term memory is good for short-term use, and long-term memory is permanently stored in the brain.

Recall: Recall is the most basic level of understanding and the lowest level of Bloom's taxonomy of understanding. If a student can recall information, she has an elementary understanding. She may not conceptualize the material, but she will be able to talk about facts she has memorized. Although not an advanced understanding, basic recall is a necessary step toward higher-level thinking.

SKILL 5.2 Understands the distinguishing features of different instructional models

SKILL 5.2.1 Describes a variety of instructional models, such as direct, indirect, independent, experiential, interactive

Direct: Direct instruction is when a teacher instructs students traditionally. Teachers will often lecture or have students answer questions. This type of learning can be useful when students are first introduced to a topic, but it should not be used too often. Students can easily become passive listeners in this type of instruction. Teachers should be careful to keep students engaged by walking around the room, asking questions, and using a conversational tone.

Indirect: Indirect instruction is student-centered. Tenets include observation, research, problem solving, and collaborative work. The teacher acts as a facilitator, not as a lecturer, and often students work together to find answers. The teacher is also there to answer questions and ensure student engagement, but the teacher's role is to help students find answers.

Independent: Independent learning often takes the form of homework or seat work, in which the student is practicing a skill or concept on her own. Often, independent learning takes place after direct or indirect instruction, and it may be appropriately scaffolded for the students needs, with the goal of students being able to complete the entire assignment on their own. Self-reflection and metacognitive practice falls under independent instruction.

> **INDIRECT:** Indirect instruction is student-centered. Tenets include observation, research, problem solving, and collaborative work. The teacher acts as a facilitator, not as a lecturer, and often students work together to find answers.

EXPERIENTIAL: This environment is student-centered and activity-based. The goal of experiential learning is not to solve a problem, but to be involved in a process.

INTERACTIVE: When a teacher is holding a full-class or small-group discussion, she is using the interactive instructional strategy.

Experiential: This environment is student-centered and activity-based. The goal of experiential learning is not to solve a problem, but to be involved in a process. Because students are actively engaged in a process, they are more likely to retain information over a long period of time.

Interactive: When a teacher is holding a full-class or small-group discussion, she is using the interactive instructional strategy. Sometimes, a teacher may use a think-pair-share activity, which is an interactive strategy because students are discussing and sharing ideas.

> Keesee, G. (2014). Instructional approaches. http://teachinglearningresources.pbworks.com/w/page/19919560/Instructional%20Approaches Retrieved Jan. 27, 2015.

SKILL 5.3 Knows a variety of instructional strategies associated with each instructional model

SKILL 5.3.1 Identifies instructional strategies associated with direct instruction, such as explicit teaching, drill and practice, lecture, demonstrations, guides for reading, listening, viewing

You will spend some of your time teaching students new material, and when you do, you may offer students new information through direct instruction. There may not always be a way to offer new material through differentiation, so prepare to do some lecturing. However, there are many ways to teach students new material, and you will most likely use all of these, depending on the type of material you are presenting.

Lecture: A teacher will have material written in PowerPoint or notes. The teacher may have a handout, and students will follow along as he moves through the notes. Keep these lectures short and to the point. Ten to fifteen minutes is the longest a lecture should go for elementary and early middle school students. Provide students with a guide to go along with the lecture and pause frequently for comprehension checks. Use colorful visuals to keep student interest and use an enthusiastic voice to engage students in active listening.

Drill and practice: Drill and practice is a traditional teacher tactic that has been used for generations. Students learn a new skill and then are given many chances to practice this skill independently. This strategy is often used in math classes, when students are assigned 30 problems to practice a skill. While drill and practice has its place, it should be used sparingly. Often, drill and practice is used for homework, morning work, or independent practice time. Make this more interesting by having students work with partners, check one another's work, or have a friendly competition.

Demonstrations: Often, a teacher will bring in materials to show a concept through a demonstration during a lecture. The demonstration will bring to life a specific concept or connect hands-on work to an abstract idea. Demonstrations work well in science, art, music, and physical education classes. Sometimes the teacher will do the demonstration himself, and other times there will be enough materials for all students to work through the manipulatives.

Guides for reading, listening, and viewing: Reading guides are manipulatives that are designed to help a child work on a certain skill. For example, some stories work on specific phonemes, and others have comprehension goals. Teachers use reading guides to help scaffold students on a certain skill such as basic recall, higher-order thinking, or sequencing.

> **SKILL 5.3.2** Identifies instructional strategies associated with indirect instruction, such as problem solving, inquiry, case studies, concept mapping, reading for meaning, cloze procedures

Often, you will not be standing in front of your class, lecturing to them about new information. In fact, you should do this as little as possible. Instead, you will focus on many types of indirect instructional strategies, through which students direct their learning using skills such as observing, shadowing, interacting, collaborating, questioning, experimenting, and drawing inferences. These strategies are student-centered, as opposed to teacher-centered. Some of the most popular are defined below:

Problem solving: Problem-based learning is often based on an authentic real-world problem. Students are given an issue and then use the knowledge they have gained in the classroom to find a solution. These problems never have one correct answer; they are open-ended to showcase students' different perspectives and give the class multiple possible solutions.

Inquiry: Students are given a question and will ask more questions, answering their questions through various methods of collecting data. Often, a teacher will use this type of indirect learning in a science class. Students will use technology, collaboration, and hands-on learning to establish an answer.

Case studies: A case study is when you give students a true or fictional story and have them use their analyzing and evaluating skills to discuss the conflict present, the solution used, the issues facing the participants, or the prevalent themes. Case studies can be used in social science, literature, or even math classes. They are authentic methods of bringing abstract concepts to life. For example, often teachers will split the class into two teams, and each team will be responsible for arguing one side of a case study. A debate or controlled class discussion can follow.

Concept mapping: Concept maps are visual aids that can be used for brainstorming, collecting, or sorting information. Sometimes they can look like spider webs, with one main idea in the middle and many details shooting out from it. Concept mapping is used to connect concepts and create a visual for similarities.

CONCEPT MAPPING:
Concept maps are visual aids that can be used for brainstorming, collecting, or sorting information.

Reading for meaning: The idea behind reading for meaning is that students should not only read to sound out words but also understand that reading is about conceptualizing ideas and learning new ideas. Reading is about connecting to the text. Students do this by looking through the text prior to reading to connect to illustrations and prior knowledge, actively searching for information during reading, and connecting to prior knowledge when reading is finished.

Cloze procedures: A cloze procedure is a literacy activity that measures reading and comprehension ability. Students will read a passage. The first sentence is complete, and after that, every few words are missing. Students will read the text individually or sometimes with the class, and then, using prediction skills, choose how to fill in the blanks.

CLOZE PROCEDURES:
A cloze procedure is a literacy activity that measures reading and comprehension ability. Students will read a passage. The first sentence is complete, and after that, every few words are missing.

> **SKILL 5.3.3** Identifies instructional strategies associated with independent instruction, such as learning contracts, research projects, learning centers, computer mediated instruction, distance learning

A teacher uses independent instruction when he wants to teach his students self-reliance, independence, and how to take initiative to solve a problem. Often, independent instruction may occur when a student or group of students needs more challenging work or when one group of students is taking an assessment and other students need an activity that provides authentic engagement. The following are examples of types of independent instruction:

Learning contracts: Learning contracts make students active participants in their learning, not just passive observers. The student is metacognitive about his learning process and knows what he needs to do to succeed. The contract lays out the expectation for both teacher and student, and both agree to what needs to be done. Often, they are written for specific assessments.

Research projects: A teacher may assign a topic or allow a student to come up with his own. The teacher may provide students with outlines, small milestones, or checklists to complete; for example, "You need to use three books, two Internet sources, and a magazine to complete your research." Students will move through the research process with some scaffolding, and teachers may set up checkpoints along the way. Research projects can be completed through a paper, presentation, or project.

Learning centers: A teacher may set up three or four learning centers in her classroom. Each one will have its own rules and supplies. The student may be responsible for checking completed items off a list or completing a project before she leaves. Or, a timer may go off signaling her to change centers. The teacher will have already taught students how to rotate centers, so she will not have to explain where students should go next. Ideally, she can be working with a small group of students while the rest of her class moves quietly through centers.

Computer-mediated instruction: When a student is learning through the use of technology, he is using computer-mediated instruction. This can refer to playing an Internet game, working on a structured computerized curriculum, or taking an online quiz through a program such as Accelerated Reader.

Distance learning: Distance learning can refer to a course or even an entire program taken over the Internet, and it is very common in home schooling and higher education programs. Students must be self-motivated and highly independent to succeed in a distance learning program, because although there are due dates and many opportunities for engagement, there will not be face-to-face interaction or as many opportunities for questions as there are in a traditional classroom setting.

SKILL 5.3.4 **Identifies instructional strategies associated with experiential and virtual instruction, such as field trips, experiments, simulations, role play, games, observations**

Experiential learning refers to learning that focuses it on the process, not just the end result. Like other learning strategies, it is focused on the learner taking an active role in the process. It is learner-centered, focusing on students doing activities such as teaching one another, collaborating, learning from the environment, or taking an active role in their learning process. The following are examples of experiential and virtual instruction:

Experiential learning refers to learning that focuses on the process, not just the end result.

Field trips: A teacher will take a group of students on a field trip when he feels they will benefit from connecting a concept learned in the classroom to a real-world context. Common field trips include places such as the zoo, an aquarium, a children's museum, a fire station, or even a show. Students can make connections between what they have learned at school and the real-life version. Often, teachers will lead up to field trips with preview activities and follow field trips with activities that help students make connections. Some teachers will even send students on treasure hunts during the field trips to ensure students see all the objectives of the day.

Experiments: Experiments often take place in science or social science classes and involve creating a hypothesis, going through a step-by-step procedure to see if the hypothesis is correct, and writing or illustrating a conclusion that examines the results and analyzes if the hypothesis was correct. Even very young students can observe or participate in experiments and may use oral discussion or create illustrations to predict what will happen during the experiment.

Simulations/role play: Although similar, these two forms of experiential learning are not the same. Both have to do with taking on roles and problem solving as a character in a certain situation, but a simulation will usually be a more familiar situation that has been practiced prior to the simulation. Role-playing is involved in simulations.

Games: Games can play a useful role in the classroom setting. Some teachers will set up a "review Jeopardy" when it is time to review for a test, and others will use games as rewards for good behavior. Games can be part of centers, as long as they review a mastered skill. Once a group of students has mastered a skill, playing a game can be an excellent reinforcement or review.

Observations: Observing a student who has mastered a skill can be a useful learning tool for another student. This is especially useful for a hands-on skill such as handwriting. One student can observe another student as she forms letters, which may help her understand what to do with her own pencil. Observing can also include watching other students complete step-by-step procedures such as math problems. Sometimes teachers will invite students to solve a problem in front of the class with the hope that others will observe and learn. Peer learning, in this case, can be an effective tool.

> **SKILL 5.3.5** Identifies instructional strategies associated with interactive instruction, such as brainstorming, cooperative learning groups, interviews, discussions, peer practice, debates

Brainstorming: Brainstorming is often done prior to beginning a unit or completing a task. Often, a teacher will lead this group in this activity, as she asks for ideas that connect to the topic. Sometimes the teacher may use a Venn diagram, or another type of graphic organizer, to help students manage their thoughts. Ideas can also be simply listed. Brainstorming can be done as a large group, as a small group, or individually. It is useful before writing an essay, looking for a solution, or deciding how to manage a task.

Cooperative learning groups: Effective group learning is not just placing students in groups and asking them to work together. Students must have specific roles and a relevant, authentic task before beginning their work so that all students are involved. For example, one student can be the discussion leader, another can provide the group with discussion questions, and yet another can keep the group on task. Additionally, a teacher may provide students a chance for peer evaluation to ensure that each student participants and no one is taking the majority of the responsibility. It is also important to teach strong communication skills prior to beginning cooperative learning groups. Active listening, trust, and making decisions are all skills needed in high-performing groups. Role-playing and games can be excellent teaching tools for ensuring that these interpersonal skills are part of a student's repertoire.

Interviews: Students can interview each other, adults in their lives, or role models to bring ideas and abstract concepts into the concrete realm. Prior to the interview, teachers can explore writing questions, asking questions, active listening, and note-taking, all important life skills. Again, role-playing could be useful in preparing for an interview. Interviews are especially useful in social science classes, but can also be used as ice breaker activities in any class. Young children can do interviews by focusing on one or two questions and reporting the answers to the class.

Discussions: A discussion is a chance for a teacher not only to get a pulse on student understanding, but also to allow students to move through new ideas and collaborate on analysis and evaluation of concepts. During a discussion, students should be facing one another so they can see and hear the participants. Additionally, teachers should not lead the discussion, but facilitate it by asking questions when needed. The teacher can also create a less formal way of sharing than the traditional hand-raising; for example, there may be a special object that the speaker holds when talking. Students may have the opportunity to pass if not interested in sharing, but active listening must be a requirement. Objectives of the class discussion should be written clearly on the board, so each student understands the reason for the conversation.

Peer practice: Peer tutoring and peer review can be effective tools in creating a higher level of understanding. Students who have mastered a skill can help a struggling student complete a worksheet. Both students will learn from this tactic. Hearing a concept from another perspective, such as a peer's, will further students' understanding.

Debates: A debate can be formal or informal. A teacher will assign positions to two teams in the class, and the groups will have time to prepare statements to argue. The debate will have an objective and often a time limit for each group of students to speak. Students can use research to prepare their statements and group collaboration. The group can choose a student in the group to make the statements. Sometimes, a teacher will encourage improvised rebuttal; other times, students will have a short time to prepare rebuttals.

What Is Cooperative Learning?
http://serc.carleton.edu/introgeo/cooperative/whatis.html
Retrieved Nov. 10, 2014.

SKILL 5.4	Knows a variety of strategies for encouraging complex cognitive processes

SKILL 5.4.1	Identifies complex cognitive processes, such as concept learning, problem solving, metacognition, critical thinking, transfer

Concept learning: Concept learning is connecting similar concepts to help student understanding. This tactic is often used in higher grade levels, when the concepts are more abstract and more difficult to understand. For example, a teacher may help students connect concept by asking for similarities across the concepts so students can connect on a deeper level. Students will work on classifying these concepts into a category as the teacher gives examples. Students can decide which fit and which do not.

Problem solving: Problem solving is a type of independent learning in which students take responsibility for how to research, plan, and solve a conflict. They will, will initial help from the teacher, understand the problem, research the details, look for various solutions, and then decide on the best course of action. Often, problem solving happens in small groups or partners to allow for collaboration. Ideas for solutions may include strategies such as creating graphic organizers, hypothesizing, making a table, finding a pattern, or working backward.

Metacognition: The simple definition of metacognition is thinking about thinking. A child who is metacognitive will think about how she learns, what she needs to gain knowledge about a concept, and why she struggles with some understanding. A person who is metacognitive takes an active role in her learning; she knows how she processes information, what type of learner she is, and the best way she can receive information. A teacher will begin early in teaching a child to be metacognitive. Self-reflections, KWL charts, and conferences with students to discuss their strengths and challenges will all help children become more metacognitive.

METACOGNITION:
Metacognition is thinking about thinking.

Critical thinking: Critical thinking is about engagement, authenticity, and giving students a chance to take control of their thinking and problem solving. Critical thinking can be used at any grade level and for any subject and is an effective way of bringing students to the higher levels of Bloom's taxonomy. Inquiry, questioning, problem solving, and collaboration are all critical thinking strategies. Critical thinking is a student-centered learning strategy that combines independent and collaborative learning to help students become better problem solvers and more metacognitive.

Transfer: Transfer is when learning about one situation affects a student's learning about a new concept. Transfer of learning can be positive or negative, depending on how the student connects to the new information. If she makes true connections from one concept to another (for example, if she correctly associates multiplication with addition), that is positive transfer. If she makes incorrect assumptions or hasn't mastered the first situation and thus makes incorrect connections to the second situation, that is negative transfer. Using background knowledge effectively by activating schema can help students create positive transfer when learning new concepts.

> **TRANSFER:** Transfer is when learning about one situation affects a student's learning about a new concept.

Concept Learning. http://www.education.com/reference/article/concept-learning/ Retrieved Oct. 10, 2014.

Problem-Solving. https://www.teachervision.com/problem-solving/teaching-methods/48451.html Retrieved Oct. 10, 2014.

Strategies to Promote Critical Thinking in the Elementary Classroom. http://www.p21.org/news-events/p21blog/1435-strategies-to-promote-critical-thinking-in-the-elementary-classroom Retrieved Oct. 10, 2014.

> **SKILL 5.4.2** Knows instructional activities specific to the development of complex cognitive processes, such as distinguishing fact from opinion, comparing and contrasting, detecting bias, predicting, categorizing, analyzing, sequencing, summarizing, inferring, decision making, evaluating, synthesizing, generalizing

Distinguishing fact from opinion *(see also Skill 2.1.1)***:** Whereas a fact is something that can be proven as true, an opinion is a subjective thought that varies from person to person. Facts are commonly accepted as correct statements, whereas opinions are not always true (although they may be popular). Facts are useful in science and math, whereas opinions are ubiquitous in the social sciences and humanities. Often, facts are used to support opinions, especially in persuasive projects such as essays and debates.

> *Whereas a fact is something that can be proven as true, an opinion is a subjective thought that varies from person to person.*

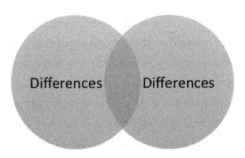

Figure 1. Venn Diagram

Comparing and contrasting: Comparing is another word for finding similarities, and contrasting is another word for finding differences. Often, it is useful to begin comparing and contrasting things by using a Venn diagram, which is a graphic organizer that shows two circles, intersecting in the middle.

The light areas represent the differences, and the darkened overlapping area represents the similarities of two concepts. This type of graphic organizer is an excellent tool for helping students begin a paper or even an oral presentation that compares and contrasts concepts.

Detecting bias: Bias is a point of view that is influenced by prior knowledge and sociocultural experiences. Everyone has biases, but often people are not aware of their own biases. If left unchecked, bias can create situations that are unfair to certain groups, even if that is not the intention. Giving examples can help students understand how bias influences decisions. For instance, if there were a vocal audition in which the judges were asked to turn around so they could not see the singers, how would that eliminate bias? Students can discuss examples like these to help determine how bias influences decisions.

Predicting: Predicting is using clues and past experiences to create a hypothesis of what will happen next. Looking through illustrations can help a young child predict what will happen in a story. Remembering how things transpired the last time an event occurred can help a child predict what will happen the next time it occurs. Additionally, teachers can use a graphic organizer, such as a KWL (what I Know, what I Want to know, and what I Learned), to help students activate prior knowledge and predict what new concepts will be introduced in a unit. Predicting is a skill that can be used in any subject at any grade level; therefore, it is useful to begin teaching how to predict as early as possible.

Categorizing: Categorizing is placing things or concepts in groups based on their similarities. Small children do this when they sort crayons by color or books by size. Older children can categorize by similarities or by definition. For example, looking through various figurative language statements, students can create categories for metaphors, similes, and so on. Young children categorize through

CATEGORIZING:
Categorizing is placing things or concepts in groups based on their similarities.

concrete senses like touch and sight, whereas older students can categorize more abstract concepts because they are higher on Bloom's taxonomy.

Analyzing: Analyzing, which is a concept on Bloom's taxonomy, is the ability to take apart a concept or event and think about every small detail to evaluate for problems and celebrate successes. Students can analyze literature, events in social science, or results of a science experiment. Teaching students to analyze an event or concept gives them the tools to explain why something happens—the reasons behind the results.

Sequencing: Sequencing is placing events in order. Young students will often do this by cutting and pasting three or four pictures in order from first to last. They will learn words such as first, next, then, and last to help them sequence. Older students may sequence steps to solving a geometric proof or any other type of math problem. They can use sequencing to work through a science experiment or to write a paper; for example, "First I brainstorm. Then I write the outline. Next, I work on the introduction, and finally, I proceed to the rough draft." Sequencing helps students create order out of chaotic concepts and organize thoughts to prepare for deeper understanding.

Summarizing: Summarizing is taking the major events, theme, and characters of a story and first creating a main idea, which succinctly describes the major lesson or theme of a piece. Next, the student will use three or four details to support his main idea statement and flesh out the summary. A summary is usually about a paragraph long and includes the main idea and three to four details. Summaries are useful because they give the reader an overview of the piece before delving into the details.

Inferring: Inferring is a higher-order thinking skill that involves drawing conclusions from hints in the text. An example of an inference is: "Although it is written clearly that the character in the short story is a boy in the third grade, the reader can infer that he is unhappy because he doesn't have any friends and spends lunch and recess by himself." Students use inference in literature and in social sciences and to predict results in science experiments. Teachers can teach young children to infer by asking them to explain what is happening in a photo or illustration, just by looking at the picture.

Decision making: Decision making is a critical thinking skill that involves autonomous problem solving. Teaching students to effectively make decisions is an important process. Explain to students how to form an opinion, support that opinion by research or facts, and clearly articulate the chosen position, without insulting or belittling others who may not agree. Students need to be aware that the decision-making process often stems from our personal experiences, and we

ANALYZING: Analyzing, which is a concept on Bloom's taxonomy, is the ability to take apart a concept or event and think about every small detail to evaluate for problems and celebrate successes.

SEQUENCING: Sequencing is placing events in order.

SUMMARIZING: Summarizing is taking the major events, theme, and characters of a story and first creating a main idea, which succinctly describes the major lesson or theme of a piece.

INFERRING: Inferring is a higher-order thinking skill that involves drawing conclusions from hints in the text.

DECISION MAKING: Decision making is a critical thinking skill that involves autonomous problem solving.

bring our prior knowledge to every decision we make. Therefore, using background schema is an important aspect of decision making.

Evaluating: Evaluating is another word for measuring. A student can evaluate the effectiveness of a source, the usefulness of a text, or the helpfulness of an assignment. Students can evaluate one another in peer evaluations or evaluate their own performances in self-evaluations. Evaluating also can be an important part of metacognition. A student should be able to understand and process his own performance in learning a new skill, and this evaluation will help him learn what he needs to gain a stronger understanding.

Synthesizing: Synthesizing is another word for putting together, or combining. It is an advanced level of comprehension that is high on Bloom's taxonomy. Keep in mind that synthesizing and summarizing, although similar, are not the same. Summarizing is identifying important information and rewriting these ideas in a paragraph, which demonstrates a lower level of understanding than synthesizing (although it can be difficult for young students). Synthesizing is not only summarizing, but also taking these ideas and creating new ideas and conclusions from the text. Often, these new ideas come from background knowledge and prior experiences, not just from the facts and statements in the text. Teachers will have to heavily scaffold this skill, especially for younger children, because it will be a challenge at first.

Generalizing: When a person generalizes information, he takes specific details and draws a conclusion that matches as many details as possible. For example, if 11 out of 15 students receive an "A" on an exam, it is plausible to generalize that the majority of the class understood the concepts tested. However, it is not a good idea to generalize based on stereotypes or biases.

> *Synthesizing.* http://www.ohiorc.org/adlit/strategy/strategy_each.aspx?id=000002 Retrieved Oct. 12, 2014.

> **EVALUATING:**
> Evaluating is another word for measuring. A student can evaluate the effectiveness of a source, the usefulness of a text, or the helpfulness of an assignment.

> **GENERALIZING:** When a person generalizes information, he takes specific details and draws a conclusion that matches as many details as possible.

SKILL 5.5 | **Knows a variety of strategies for supporting student learning**

Students all come to the classroom with their own sociocultural contexts, prior knowledge, and academic background. Additionally, they all have their own learning styles. When a teacher creates a lesson plan, he needs to differentiate his instruction and use as many teaching strategies as possible to help students understand the concepts. Use direct instruction when necessary, but, when possible, and when teaching in small groups or when using guided instruction, use one of the following teaching strategies instead:

SKILL 5.5.1 Identifies and explains uses of strategies for supporting student learning, such as modeling, developing self-regulation skills, scaffolding, differentiating instruction, guided practice, coaching

Modeling: When a teacher models for her students, she gives explicit instructions on how to handle a concept and then gives step-by-step directions, which the class follows together. It may be important to use visual cues, such as various colors when changing steps or graphic organizers, or allow students to use highlighters to help them stay on track. Keep students engaged during the modeling; they should not just be passive observers. Have them move through the problem or process with you, so they see each step as it happens. Speaking the steps aloud is a very important part of modeling. The teacher should say each step as she does it and have the class repeat as they perform the task.

> MODELING: When a teacher models for her students, she gives explicit instructions on how to handle a concept and then gives step-by-step directions, which the class follows together.

Self-regulation skills: Self-regulation skills are similar to metacognitive skills. They develop in young children and are evident in children who behave in a similar way whether they are being watched by an adult or playing independently. For example, a child who is told not to hit but does so as soon as an adult leaves the room does not have self-regulation skills. Although she follows the rules when adults are watching, she cannot remember and follow these rules when alone. An older child will exhibit self-regulation skills when she acts in control of her learning environment. She will understand that challenges are present to help her, and know what she needs to do to be successful.

> Self-regulatory skills are connected to intrinsic motivation. When a child self-regulates her learning, she understands why she is in school, what she needs to succeed, what her challenges are, and how she needs to manage her time and understanding so she can master presented concepts.

Self-regulation is a precursor to many important school skills, such as attentiveness and general school readiness. Preschoolers spend time in a pretend world, creating their own games with their own rules. In these games, are learning how to self-regulate as they learn how to follow the rules they have invented.

Scaffolding: Scaffolding is a term made popular by Lev Vygotsky when he discussed the zone of proximal development. When a teacher scaffolds, he is helping a student complete a task that the student eventually will be responsible for completing on his own. A teacher who is scaffolding correctly will break up a large skill into smaller parts, teach each part, practice each part, and watch for student mastery. When mastery is attained, the student can learn the next piece. For example, if a first-grade teacher takes students on a "picture walk" to predict what will happen in a story, then helps them find the sight words they already know how to read, and finally asks them to circle any words they don't know, he is preparing them to read the story as a whole by first breaking it down into parts.

> SCAFFOLDING: When a teacher scaffolds, he is helping a student complete a task that the student eventually will be responsible for completing on his own.

Differentiating instruction: Differentiating instruction is a term for dividing instruction based on student need and student learning style. In a classroom, there may be various small-group learning centers, each with a similar objective but a

> DIFFERENTIATING INSTRUCTION: Differentiating instruction is a term for dividing instruction based on student need and student learning style.

distinctive way of teaching the objective. For example, while some students may work with a teacher and receive direct instruction on a new concept, others may listen to a recording of a story and fill out a worksheet. Other students may be asked to play a matching game to reinforce a particular concept, and others may be using a computer to reinforce the concept. A teacher will create centers based on various learning styles such as visual, auditory, kinesthetic, interpersonal, and musical. Differentiating instruction also has to do with meeting students at their academic level. Whereas some students may need an extra challenge, others may need remediation. It is up to the teacher to find the right lesson for each of his students to challenge their knowledge and bring them to the next level.

Guided practice: Guided practice is the step following modeling. In this step, teachers call on students to help with the process. Give students an opportunity to help others so they don't feel uncomfortable being put on the spot. Consider calling not only on students who are volunteering, but also on those who have knowledge and understanding in the area. Keep other students engaged during guided practice by asking the whole class to vocalize the steps, and use different colors to represent the steps as you move through them together.

> *Guided practice is the step following modeling.*

Coaching: A teacher who uses a coaching instructional strategy recognizes that each child has his own learning style and that learning is a process. A "coach" will help each child set individual goals and work toward these goals, check in with the child to make sure understanding is happening, and provide feedback to make sure the child is engaged and progressing in her learning. A "coach" is supportive and positive and deals with challenges in the most respectful way possible, creating a nurturing and safe environment in the classroom. A "coach" will use various instructional methods, such as direct instruction and scaffolding, to help the child move forward in her knowledge.

"Coaching for Success in the Classroom" https://www.nde-ed.org/TeachingResources/ClassroomTips/Coaching_for_Success.htm Retrieved Nov. 12, 2014.

Herrmann, E. "The importance of guided practice in the classroom" (2014). http://exclusive.multibriefs.com/content/the-importance-of-guided-practice-in-the-classroom Retrieved Nov. 12, 2014.

Self-regulation http://www.toolsofthemind.org/philosophy/self-regulation/ Retrieved Nov. 12, 2014.

SKILL 5.6 Knows basic strategies for promoting students' development of self-regulatory skills

Self-regulatory skills begin in toddlerhood. When we tell a toddler to wait one minute before we read that story to him or to wait for us to finish a load of laundry before we build a tower, we are teaching him to self-regulate. By not always answering a toddler's requests immediately, we are teaching him to be patient and to have control over his environment. Older children need self-regulatory skills to succeed in school. Self-regulatory skills are connected to intrinsic motivation. When a child self-regulates her learning, she understands why she is in school, what she needs to succeed, what her challenges are, and how she needs to manage her time and understanding so she can master presented concepts. Teachers can help students become more self-regulatory by using the strategies discussed in the next section.

SKILL 5.6.1 Knows how to support students in setting goals, managing time, organizing information, monitoring progress, reflecting on outcomes, establishing a productive work environment

How does a teacher help a student self-regulate? Ideally, students are engaged in the material, so their motivation comes from within. To accomplish this, assignments needs to be authentic and important to each learner.

Teaching self-regulation begins in understanding where the student is and where she needs to be. Invite the student to a short conference, during which you can set academic goals together. How long will it take to reach these goals? What small steps will the student take to become more confident with his new knowledge? Together, the teacher and student can set up a timetable, where the student is responsible for certain assessments at certain times to make sure he is managing time well. Additionally, the student can do periodic self-assessments and journal entries to measure his own progress and sharpen his metacognitive skills.

Of course, the student needs to function in a productive work environment. What does that look like? Usually a productive work environment has little noise, materials ready to go, a teacher willing to help when necessary, ng any independent work or assessments. The instructor should be available for scaffolding or mentoring when necessary. The self-regulated learner is not on his own; rather, he is learning to become independent with the help of his teacher.

SKILL 5.6.2 Understands the design of different group configurations for learning

Although every student learns differently, as evidenced in Howard Gardner's multiple intelligences, students will learn better in different configurations. While some students thrive on the large-group atmosphere, others get lost and are better off in a small group or even by themselves. It's important not to force students to work in a configuration that is going to cause them to fail. It is acceptable to encourage students to work outside their comfort zone on occasion, but if a student becomes severely anxious because he has been asked to work in a group, perhaps allowing him to work on his own may be preferable. In the next section, we will discuss common group configurations in a classroom.

SKILL 5.6.3 Describes different group configurations, such as whole-class, small-group, independent learning, one-on-one, pair/share

Whole-class: Whole-class configuration is the most common configuration and the easiest for the teacher in terms of preparation. The teacher creates one lesson, and the whole class participates. Whole-class instruction is particularly useful when introducing a new topic, using direct instruction, using lecture, or giving a whole-class assessment.

Small-group: Small-group learning often takes place at centers where students can work on various objectives. Usually, one of these centers includes working with a teacher on a skill. Often, the teacher will create various lesson plans that will match the ability of each small group, so each group is challenged.

Independent learning: When a child is working independently, he is practicing a skill on his own. Usually this type of learning strategy comes after group practice and guided practice, and it is useful only if the student is somewhat proficient in the skill. Homework, assessments, and bell work are all examples of independent work.

One-on-one: One-on-one teaching is useful especially when a student is in need of remediation. Peer tutoring and teacher/student tutoring are all examples of one-on-one instruction. One-on-one instruction can go at the student's own pace, pausing when necessary and speeding up when the student shows proficiency.

The think-pair-share strategy gives students time to think about a concept, discuss it with a partner, and then share their ideas with the class.

Pair/share: The think-pair-share strategy gives students time to think about a concept, discuss it with a partner, and then share their ideas with the class. The think-pair-share strategy works like this: first, a teacher poses a question, usually a relatively difficult higher-order thinking question that includes words like synthesize, analyze, or evaluate. Students are given a few moments to think about this question on their own. Next, they discuss their thoughts with partners. Often, the teacher pairs students to ensure various skill levels are met. Finally, one person from each group shares the group answer with the class, and this evolves into a whole-class discussion.

SKILL 5.7 Understands the use and implications of different grouping techniques and strategies

When you are working with students, you may choose to create lessons in which students sometimes are working on their own and sometimes working together. You may choose to group students by ability in certain situations, or even by gender or age. These groupings can make certain types of learning a priority.

SKILL 5.7.1 Explains the uses, strengths, and limitations of a variety of grouping techniques, such as cooperative learning, collaborative learning, heterogeneous grouping, homogeneous grouping, multi-age grouping, grouping by gender

Collaborative learning/cooperative learning: Collaborative learning environments are rooted in Vygotsky's idea that learning takes place in a society. Anything that students do together is called collaborative learning. Students are working together toward a goal and helping one another along the way, using background knowledge to help solve problems. Cooperative learning is a type of collaborative learning. In a cooperative learning environment, students work in groups to accomplish a goal and use each other's strengths to complete the task. The task is not usually something small; rather, it involves higher-order thinking such as analyzing, evaluating, and synthesizing. Usually a group grade is given, rather than an individual grade, based on how well the group completes the task. Students learn to ask questions of one another, and the teacher acts as a facilitator, answering questions when needed but often just leading students toward the right answer.

Heterogeneous grouping: When students are grouped heterogeneously, students of many levels are represented in each group. Often, students with a higher level of understanding can help students who have a lower level of understanding.

Homogeneous grouping: In a homogeneous classroom, students are all within the same academic level. Often, a gifted class will be homogeneously grouped, because those students have all tested into the class and need to be challenged.

When students are grouped heterogeneously, students of many levels are represented in each group.

In a homogeneous classroom, students are all within the same academic level.

Additionally, there are remediation classes in which all the students struggle with similar concepts. Grouping students based on similar academic skill can ensure that they continue to be challenged.

Multi-age grouping/grouping by gender: Students are sometimes grouped in multi-age groups during physical education classes. Often, a third-grade class with have PE with a fourth-grade class, which helps the younger students follow the older students in physical ability. Because students move around during PE and are not expected to perform in a specific way, multi-age grouping can be beneficial. Mentoring and coaching also can take place in PE class, so the multi-age group can work well in this environment.

Sometimes, grouping by gender is acceptable. Often, children in health classes will be grouped by gender to avoid embarrassing situations during delicate conversations. Additionally, some research has shown that in academic settings, girls have a tendency not to share as often when there are males present; intimidation or wanting to impress the boys may be a factor.

SKILL 5.8	Knows how to select an appropriate strategy for achieving an instructional objective

What should students learn by the end of each mini-lesson? By the end of each day? By the end of each unit? A teacher should ask herself these questions as she plans her instruction and assessments. She will plan an assessment based on what she'd like her students to know, and her strategy for instructional objectives should be oriented toward achieving goals and understanding.

Questions the educator should ask herself as she chooses a strategy for instruction may include: What do my students know how to do now (prior to the lesson)? What should they be able to do once the lesson is complete? How will the learning environment look? What will be the change in my students' knowledge? How will this new knowledge be evaluated? What level of proficiency will be acceptable?

Once the educator knows the answers to these questions, he can begin lesson planning. For example, if the teacher is looking for minimal proficiency, a quick mini-lesson with a formative assessment may be satisfactory. However, if he is looking for mastery learning, the lesson may last for days. Small-group instruction may be necessary, especially if the goal is to get most students to a high level of proficiency. The teacher's strategy should address as many of the objectives as possible. Choosing direct instruction over cooperative learning, for example, may be best in a time crunch and may provide the fastest route to understanding, even though it provides fewer opportunities for higher-order thinking activities. Teachers must prioritize objectives and plan accordingly.

Assessment primer: Writing instructional objectives.
http://assessment.uconn.edu/primer/objectives1.html
Retrieved Jan. 5, 2015.

SKILL 5.9 Understands the concept of monitoring and adjusting instruction in response to student feedback

SKILL 5.9.1 Explains the instructional purposes of monitoring and adjusting instruction

Teachers monitor instruction to determine if their students are reaching the set objectives. Are they receiving the information in an appropriate context? Are they understanding the information, or are they just memorizing it? Formative assessments will be the key to measuring student progress because they monitor not only student understanding, but also teacher effectiveness. Is the teacher reaching every student? Sometimes, students need to be monitored individually because their progress and understanding will happen at different paces.

Monitoring student instruction will be a key to adjusting teacher instruction. If students are struggling with a particular aspect of a concept, and the teachers sees this challenge through a formative assessment, she can reteach the concept in a new way before the unit has moved too far beyond the initial concept.

Additionally, if a teacher is continuously monitoring her students, he can catch student pitfalls before they become too large and difficult to correct. The teacher's next step, after realizing that students do not understand the concepts, would be to adjust instruction. Perhaps he works with small groups, creates a collaborative learning activity, or incorporates an authentic project that weaves in the new concepts.

SKILL 5.9.2 Knows strategies for monitoring and adjusting instruction

Sometimes a teacher will plan a lesson, and then, to her dismay, it will quickly become a disaster. Rarely will students say they are disinterested or do not understand the concept. Instead, they may misbehave; become silly, unfocused, or disengaged; or refuse to stay on task. These are all examples of student feedback, and sometimes, depending on the severity of the student reaction, the teacher may choose to adjust her lesson immediately. There are many ways to adjust instruction; for example, move from whole group to small group, devise a quick kinesthetic activity for muscle memory, or stop the lesson entirely and make a new plan that evening.

Often, student feedback will come in the form of performance on an assessment. If the mean score is lower than average—or even just about average—and the teacher was expecting a high proficiency level, he needs to reteach the concept, most likely in a new way. Perhaps the students didn't understand the concept, felt the assessment did not appropriately match the taught content, or did not receive enough instructional time. Although a teacher should take note of student understanding during formative assessments, it may take low scores on a summative assessment for him to notice that his students do not understand the concept.

SKILL 5.10	**Recognizes the purpose of reflecting upon, analyzing, and evaluating the effectiveness of instructional strategies**

Without reflection, a teacher will not grow. A teacher needs to understand what she has done well, what she has done wrong, and how different populations of students can benefit from different instructional strategies.

How does a teacher evaluate and analyze his instructional strategy? He may begin by looking at summative test scores, analyzing data, seeing which skills students struggle with, and focusing instruction on necessary skill-building activities. Additionally, the teacher should measure his effectiveness against student engagement and enthusiasm to learn. Students who are happy and motivated will be more likely to trust the instructor, learn, and apply new concepts.

Reflection can also come in the form of talking with a peer, mentor, or coach; writing in a journal; analyzing past lessons and comparing them to present ones; or even just thinking about the challenges each day brings. Reflection does not always take place after the lesson. A strong teacher will reflect before she brings a lesson to her class, trying to pinpoint the places students will struggle and devising preemptive strategies to manage these difficulties.

Sometimes, a teacher may even record his lesson, much like an athlete records his game, to notice his strengths and weaknesses. This type of reflecting can be honest, and it can be game-changing if a peer or mentor views it. Perhaps the follow-up conversation can be on strategies to handle similar challenges in the future.

SKILL 5.11 Knows the characteristics of different types of memory and their implications for instructional planning and student learning

---

SKILL 5.11.1 Distinguishes among the different types of memory, such as short term and long term *(see also Skills 4.2.1 and 5.1)*

Short-term memory: Short-term memory is the small amount of information that we can store for a very short period of time. There is a reason why most phone numbers are seven numbers—most people can store around seven items at a time in their short-term memory. Information that is placed in the short-term memory is quickly lost unless a person makes an effort to move the information into long-term memory.

Long-term memory: Memorization exercises, experiences, or conceptualizations help a student commit an idea or concept to longer-term memory, which is more permanent storage than short-term memory. Often, a person will use background schema to match new information and be able to recall it quickly. Mnemonic devices are an example of using prior knowledge to connect new knowledge to long-term memory.

SKILL 5.11.2 Considers the characteristics and effects of memory on student learning when planning instruction

Short-term memory only lasts 10 to 15 seconds; therefore, rote memorization without practice is not going to give students any lasting information. Instead, teachers should spend time giving students guided and independent practice so they can become comfortable with the concepts, not just the facts. This is where collaborative learning, differentiated instruction such as centers, independent practice, and even homework can help a student retain concepts. Also, remember to continue to review familiar concepts throughout the year. If a concept is discussed once and then forgotten, students will have a much smaller chance of remembering it than if they are given many opportunities for practice and connections throughout the year. The goal is to ensure that new concepts are pulled into a child's background schema so that they become part of prior knowledge for the next new concept.

SKILL 5.12 **Recognizes the role of teachable moments in instruction**

SKILL 5.12.1 **Defines and provides examples of a teachable moment**

SKILL 5.12.2 **Understands the uses of the teachable moment**

> *A teachable moment is a moment that the teacher did not anticipate; a moment that he may not have placed in his lesson plan but that occurs during discussion or, often, right before instruction begins.*

A teachable moment is a moment that the teacher did not anticipate; a moment that he may not have placed in his lesson plan but that occurs during discussion or, often, right before instruction begins. The teacher needs to be aware of these moments, because they are fleeting and easy to miss. They are often tangential and may not have anything to do with the academic topic at hand, but they are important for student learning. For example, in a social studies class, a planned discussion about cultural differences could turn into a teachable moment about tolerance. Perhaps a student makes a comment about how many cultures are different and sometimes it is difficult to see why certain cultures have the traditions that they do. The teacher can broaden this comment by asking the class what traditions in their own culture might seem uncomfortable for others, and if the teacher is able to steer the conversation correctly and manage such a delicate topic with grace, the students may complete the class understanding why tolerance is such an important quality to have.

Teachable moments don't always come during class. For example, a teacher may overhear a student saying that another student is stupid because she doesn't ever know the right answer. Although this type of comment may seem outside the teacher's jurisdiction, it is not. A teacher could begin her class with a quick activity that pulls in student attention and explains why a safe and nurturing classroom is so important. She may choose to focus on why trying is more important than being correct and how if we don't try or never fail, we will never grow.

Teachable moments are usually quick and unintentional comments made by students, but a professional educator will recognize these moments as just as important as his academic standards and will make room in his day for them—even if it is only a few minutes. Students also need to know that teachers are noticing them, even when they are not speaking in an academic context. When teachers discuss these off-topic moments with students, children understand that their instructors are paying attention to them all the time, even when it is not obvious.

COMPETENCY 6
QUESTIONING TECHNIQUES

> SKILL **Knows the components of effective questioning, such as allowing**
> 6.1 **think/wait time, helping students articulate their ideas, respecting**
> **students' answers, handling incorrect answers, encouraging**
> **participation, establishing a non-critical classroom environment,**
> **promoting active listening, varying the types of questions**

Allowing think/wait time: It is very important for a teacher to allow an appropriate amount of time before asking students to answer her question. Sometimes, waiting as long as 20 seconds will be necessary. During this time, the teacher can ask students to write their answer in a journal. Younger students can sketch a picture of their answer so they do not forget their thought. Some students may know the answer right away, but others will need the full wait time, so it is important not to call on the first child who raises his hand. This will interrupt the thought process of the other students, and these students may never reach the answer on their own if another student has already given the answer to the instructor. These students who needed more wait time may give up on even trying, because they know someone else will answer.

Helping students articulate their ideas/promoting active listening: Some students may have difficulty articulating their ideas, while other students will be very verbal. If a student needs more time to speak, give her that time. Do not interrupt her while she articulates her thought and do not allow other students to interrupt her. Additionally, some students may find it easier to write their answer, draw their answer, or even fill out a graphic organizer and then verbalize when they have their thoughts together.

Encourage active listening by teaching students what active listening is. An active listener looks at the speaker, does not engage in any other activity, and shows he understands by repeating what the speaker has said in his own words. For example, if the speaker is discussing why he felt left out at recess, an active listener can respond by saying, "You felt sad at recess because no one asked you to play on the swings?" Then the speaker can validate that answer. Use examples that children will understand when explaining what an active listener looks like. This will help them identify with the situation and remember how to react in a similar situation.

Respecting students' answers/establishing a noncritical classroom environment: A safe classroom environment will be key to students feeling self-confident and respected. How does a teacher create such an environment? Initially, she establishes rules that encourage respect and kindness. Post these rules on the classroom wall as a constant visual reminder. Additionally, teach students how to be respectful of others' opinions, even when they don't agree. For example, "I don't agree," could be changed to, "I understand what you're saying, but I have a different idea." Teachers should model respect for students at all times and refrain from yelling or losing control. If there is a behavior management chart available on which students can move their name down a color if they choose to break a rule, the teacher will not have to constantly remind her students to follow rules or make good choices.

Handling incorrect answers: Students will try for the right answer, but they will not always be right. The instructor must handle this situation delicately so as not to injure the child's self-confidence and to encourage future participation. For example, a teacher should not say, "That is wrong." A teacher should also not say, "Incorrect. Next?" Instead, a teacher should help the student reach the correct answer by using Socratic questioning, guiding the student toward the right answer through restating the student's thought and asking more questions. For example, "You have guessed that the answer is five. How did you reach that answer?" The student may point to his work or verbally explain his process. At this point, the teacher can find the missing piece: "Are you sure three plus one is five? Why don't we check that again with these blocks?" Sometimes a teacher may encourage students to "phone a friend": they can ask a classmate for help on an answer. This will only work if the friend can explain the correct process. Just giving the answer will not teach the student how to find the solution on his own. Instead, aide him in becoming more independent so he can eventually work toward the solution on his own.

Encouraging participation: Often, the same types of students will raise their hands. These are usually the students who quickly know the answer, who are confident in their skills, or who don't mind being wrong. While it is important to encourage these students, it is also necessary to give each child a chance to participate. Keep in mind that not every child wants to answer aloud. Some may prefer speaking in small groups or writing down their answer, and others may work best in a one-on-one atmosphere. All of these students are participating, but in their own comfort zone. As long as the instructor knows each child's level of understanding, not every child needs to participate in every discussion.

However, a teacher can encourage children to step out of their comfort zone if he has established a safe environment. For example, perhaps the class is split into three groups for playing a review game for a test. Each group member gets a popsicle stick of a different color. The teacher asks a review question, and the whole group has one minute to choose an answer and tell everyone in their group. When the timer goes off, the teacher chooses one color, and the person holding that colored popsicle stick in each group is the spokesperson for that question. In this situation, everyone has already been given the answer, so a student who is uncomfortable speaking to the group may feel more confident because she has the support of her entire group.

Varying the types of questions: Questions and answers can vary. From lower-level recall questions to higher-order thinking questions, the way a teacher asks a question can build student confidence and help students conceptualize information. For example, when asking questions about a story and testing comprehension, beginning with simple yes/no questions can ease children into their answers; for example, "Did the story take place during the daytime? Was the main character a girl?" These questions are using important comprehension vocabulary words but are phrased in a non-intimidating way. After students answer these types of questions, the teacher can move on to broader questions: "What was the name of the main character? Where was the setting? Can you describe the plot?" The next level of questioning is higher-order thinking, which involves more than basic recall. These questions will use words such as why, how, and, for older students, analyze and evaluate. For example, "How did the conflict resolve?" or "Can you analyze the main character's choices in the first half of the story and predict what will happen next?" Give students a chance to answer these questions in a way that is comfortable for them. Answering aloud, think-pair-share, illustrations, and journaling are all appropriate ways to answer questions.

SKILL 6.2	Understands the uses of questioning

SKILL 6.2.1	Explains and provides different examples of different purposes of questioning, such as developing interest and motivating students, evaluating students' preparation, reviewing previous lessons, helping students set realistic expectations, engaging students in discussion, determining prior knowledge, preparing students for what is to be learned, guiding thinking, developing critical and creative thinking skills, checking for comprehension or level of understanding, summarizing information, stimulating students to pursue knowledge on their own

Developing interest and motivating students: An excellent way to develop student interest is to find out what students know and what interests them and then connect the lesson to their likes and background knowledge. Incorporating KWL charts and activating prior knowledge through allowing students to tell stories of their own experiences will motivate them to learn more about a subject. Additionally, encouraging student-directed learning will increase students' motivation. Teachers should use minimal direct instruction and then give students tasks, ability to research, tools to find answers, and time to work collaboratively. Having ownership over authentic assignments is an excellent way to ensure student motivation.

Evaluating students' preparation: How do teachers know how ready students are to begin learning new concepts? A teacher can look formally at a student's scores on previous assessments to determine what she knows and how prepared she is for the next level of understanding. Teachers also give pretests for this reason. Informally, the teacher should also talk to a student's past teachers to figure out the student's strengths and weaknesses. Finally, if a student has attained metacognitive skills, the teacher can ask a student to fill out a self-assessment or even have a conference with the student, evaluating the student's preparation and skill level.

Reviewing previous lessons: Before beginning a new unit, it's important to review what you have already taught the students so they remember where to begin their new knowledge and which background schema to activate. There are many ways to do this, including using a KWL chart (more on this later in this section), using a self-reflection rubric, using a prior knowledge checklist, having a classroom discussion, or making a graphic organizer with students. Regardless of which strategy you choose, this is a critical piece of a new lesson. Students will not be able to frame their learning if they are unable to put it in a familiar context.

Helping students set realistic expectations: What will students learn in a lesson? Setting goals and objectives for each day and week can help students understand what they will be learning. Write these goals and objectives on the board and explain them. Objectives may be short term, while goals will be more long term. Some teachers also write the assessment on the board so students understand how and when they will have to demonstrate their new knowledge. Repeat the objective as the lesson continues so students know why they are learning. For example, if the class is studying money, the teacher can say, "Because our objective today is to identify the difference between a quarter and a dime, we are going to play a game that helps us learn the differences." When the teacher sets goals for each lesson and objectives for each unit, students will feel that they can accomplish what is being asked of them, and they may feel less intimidated.

Some students may need to be challenged, and for them goals and objectives may be different. Differentiated instruction will be important when creating goals and objectives and expectations for learning. Not every student will have the same expectation for learning.

Engaging students in discussion: Some students will naturally want to be a part of discussion. They will raise their hand each time the teacher asks and will answer teacher questions without reservation. However, other students will be shier. Some may not want to participate because they are nervous about answering incorrectly, and others may feel that their peers may laugh at their answer. Still others may not have enough time to process the question before a faster classmate answers it. Combat these frustrations by giving at least 20 seconds of "think" time before calling on a student. Additionally, ask students to write down what they think the answer may be, even if they don't share it with the class. The students who are correct and see it on their paper will gain more confidence, and soon they may want to volunteer their answer. Alternatively, consider asking questions during small-group instruction to encourage nervous or shy students to participate.

Finally, some teachers choose to call on students who rarely participate to draw them out, rather than call on students who participate often. This can be a good strategy if other students are prepared to answer—a teacher must never require students to answer a question orally in front of a large group. This can cause severe anxiety for some students and will be more detrimental than productive.

Determining prior knowledge/preparing students for what is to be learned:
Before beginning a lesson, a teacher must find out what his students already know and explain the objective of the lesson. One way to do this is to use a KWL chart. A KWL chart is set up with three columns and looks like this:

WHAT I KNOW	WHAT I WANT TO KNOW	WHAT I LEARNED

Before beginning the lesson, the teacher will explain the unit. For example, "We are going to start talking about volcanoes. Does anyone know anything about volcanoes?" Students may start talking about lava, mountains, or other phenomena of nature. The teacher can write these in the "What I Know" column. Next, the students can discuss, first in a small group and then with the class, what they would like to know about volcanoes. The teacher than places this chart on the wall of the classroom for the duration of the unit. At the end of the unit, the class goes back to the chart and together writes in what they have learned about volcanoes during this time. This type of exercise gives students ownership over the unit and helps them connect their prior knowledge to what they have learned during the lessons. Activating prior knowledge also helps students become meta-cognitive, because as students see how prior incorporate new concepts into their long-term memory.

Guiding thinking/developing critical and creative thinking skills: Critical thinking involves using logic, analysis, synthesis, and evaluation to create solutions, be persuasive, or support opinions with sound arguments. These are all higher-order thinking skills, but they can be taught at a very young age. For example, teachers should not just accept the right answer; they always should ask a student how she came to the right answer. Discussing the process involves critical thinking. Additionally, making predictions through looking at illustrations or patterns can help a student analyze what will come next. If possible, allow a child to come to the answer in his own way, even if the explanation is not what you expect. Allow students to explore, be hands-on, and be problem solvers by activating their prior knowledge, giving them a task, and allowing them to discover.

Checking for comprehension or level of understanding: Checking for comprehension can be a difficult task because not all students will be able to perform on assessments, even if they understand exactly what they have read. Therefore, it is important to have multiple strategies to check understanding. For example, verbally check understanding by pausing as the class reads to ask questions like: "Can someone tell me why this character was happy?" or "What do we know so far about the setting of the story?" Creating checkpoints will give the teacher a chance to see if students are understanding or if the class needs to go back and reread the information. Older students can write notes in margins to remind them of important details as they read. Students can draw pictures, discuss details with partners, or complete short worksheets or graphic organizers that will check understanding.

Summarizing information: To create a summary, students pull the most important facts and statements out of a piece of work and then rephrase them in their own words. The student should be able to tell the story of what happened, without stumbling on insignificant details. This can be difficult for young students because to do it correctly, they must be able to pull out information that is necessary to tell the story. Help students with this by using highlighters as they read. Teachers can show students how to highlight important statements or circle important passages that explain critical details such as characters, setting, conflict, and plot.

Stimulating students to pursue knowledge on their own: Students will pursue knowledge when they feel ownership of the task and motivation to learn more. Students want to know why the information is important and how it connects to experiences in the real world. Worksheets and homework assignments that can be categorized as "busy work"—work that is just assigned to keep students occupied—is not going to motivate them to pursue knowledge on their own. In contrast, an assignment that activates their background schema and excites them about their own lives will encourage them to learn independently. For example, when studying a historical event such as the events of September 11, instead of asking students to fill out a worksheet, it may be more authentic to have students ask their parents what they remember about the day. Students can share these experiences in school, and then make a chart that examines the collective answers.

SKILL 6.3 Knows strategies for supporting students in articulating their ideas

SKILL 6.3.1 Explains and provides examples of strategies for supporting students in articulating their ideas, such as verbal and non-verbal prompting, restatement, reflective listening statements, wait time

Verbal and nonverbal prompting: Verbal cues include the words we use; non-verbal cues are all other aspects of communication. The lack of nonverbal cues often makes email and texting communication difficult. A teacher needs to be aware of all the signals she is sending her students through her nonverbal cues. For example, tone of voice, body language, eye contact, and facial expressions are all nonverbal cues. If a teacher wants a child to continue speaking, he may smile at the child. If the teacher is frustrated with him, he may give him "The Look," a familiar face of intimidation, and the child will stop his behavior. Teachers should model active listening by engaging in eye contact, smiling, and using welcoming body language to help students feel safe and nurtured.

Restatement/reflective listening statements: To be an active listener, a person must be able to respond well and show the speaker he is listening. Restating what the person has said is an excellent start. For example, when a child tells a teacher she is afraid of another student, the teacher should not respond by saying, "Don't worry. It will be fine." An active listener would instead say, "I hear that you are afraid of Chloe. Can you tell me more about that?" When the child goes on to explain that Chloe says makes fun of her clothes, the teacher can respond by saying, "You are afraid of Chloe because she laughs at you because of what you wear. Is that right?" By restating the child's concern, the teacher makes the child feels validated and heard. The teacher can then help the child come up with a solution.

Wait time: When a question is asked of children, they should be given at least 20 seconds to answer. Some students may not require wait time, but others will require more than 20 seconds. Students who are rushing to answer can be asked to wait patiently or to write their answer in a journal so they do not forget. Allow students to move through their thought processes without interruption so they can come to a conclusion on their own without being told by a faster and perhaps more impulsive peer.

SKILL 6.4 Knows methods for encouraging higher levels of thinking

SKILL 6.4.1 Explains and provides examples of methods for encouraging students' higher levels of thinking, thereby guiding students to reflect, challenge assumptions, find relationships, determine relevancy and validity of information, design alternative solutions, draw conclusions, transfer knowledge

Higher-order thinking means moving past basic understanding into conceptualizing. Students will do more than explain basic facts—they will take the facts and explore how they fit into a bigger, more abstract picture.

The first step in encouraging higher-order thinking is to have thoughtful conversations with students. Avoid the easy questions and the questions with a yes/no answer. Instead, ask questions that encourage students to analyze, evaluate, and synthesize information. Drawing conclusions, making inferences, and making predictions are all higher-order thinking skills that can be practiced in even the most casual conversation.

Second, collaborative and cooperative learning are higher-order thinking opportunities. Activities such as giving groups a dilemma to solve or asking them to develop an argument, solve a logic puzzle, or apply their classroom knowledge to authentic situations will practice higher-order thinking skills.

When giving students an assignment, whether it is individual or collaborative, keep in mind that the questions should require them to do more than just memorize facts. Memorizing and basic understanding is the lowest level of comprehension. To practice higher-order thinking skills, the activity should ask the student to predict, evaluate, diagram, describe, compare, or interpret.

SKILL 6.5 Knows strategies for promoting a safe and open forum for discussion

Without a safe and nurturing environment, students will not be comfortable sharing their thoughts, being incorrect, or supporting others' opinions. The following section will give a brief overview of techniques and strategies for creating and maintaining a supportive and nurturing classroom.

SKILL 6.5.1 Knows basic techniques for establishing and maintaining standards of conduct for discussions, such as engaging all learners, creating a collaborative environment, respecting diverse opinions, supporting risk taking

When a teacher begins a class discussion, he should first set ground rules. Active listening, full engagement, raising hand to speak, and patiently waiting to be called on are all appropriate rules. Students who get impatient may always write down what they would like to say so they don't forget while they wait their turn. Once the discussion begins, the teacher acts as a facilitator. He will ask questions and guide the students to various answers, using Socratic questioning and encouraging the entire class to participate. Some students may be shy and may not want to participate, so the teacher can incorporate a "pass" if the child feels extremely uncomfortable. Some students may even benefit from some extrinsic motivation to encourage them to participate. A teacher can walk around with stickers and give out a sticker each time a student participates. Most students will enjoy collecting little prizes and may even put all the stickers on their paper to show their participation.

If there are many shy students in a class, the teacher could begin the class discussion with a think-pair-share activity to help students identify their opinions. If students come prepared to the discussion, they will feel more confident in their answers and may be more likely to participate when the whole class is asked to share.

Taking risks is part of having a discussion, and not all students will agree all the time. However, everyone should feel safe to share, even if what they say is not popular. Student opinions will vary, and it is important for students to know how to respect one another, even when they disagree. Students can debate one another's answers but should always validate other students' opinions. For example, a student may say, "You said you liked the choice the main character made because you think he is brave, but actually, I disagree. I think what he did makes him a coward." Other students can weigh in on both opinions.

Discussions can be useful for class learning. They put the students in charge of their learning, and are just the type of student-directed activity that can foster collaboration, respect, and the development of new ideas.

COMPETENCY 7
COMMUNICATION TECHNIQUES

> **SKILL 7.1** Understands various verbal and nonverbal communication modes

If a student does not trust her teacher, the student will not learn anything from the teacher. Fortunately, a teacher is creating trust with her students every time she interacts with them. Although she will be talking with them all day, it is extremely important for her to be aware of her nonverbal cues. Nonverbal cues, such as body language, gestures, tone, and eye contact, will establish a foundation for how students react to her and whether they consider her to be approachable or intimidating.

> **SKILL 7.1.1** Explains and provides examples of body language; gesture; tone, stress, and inflection; eye contact; facial expression; personal space

Body language/gesture: Open body language includes keeping hands by the sides, facing the speaker, and engaging in eye contact. Closed body language includes crossing arms, turning away from the speaker, or looking down or away from the speaker. If a teacher uses closed body language, he should not expect students to feel comfortable speaking with him. Instead, students may feel afraid and nervous to approach him with an issue.

Body language and gestures are very important to teacher/student communication. For example, if a teacher stands in front of students with her arms crossed, the students will feel aloofness and anger. If she stands with her hands by her sides or gestures while speaking to show enthusiasm, the students will be more active listeners and more excited to learn. The energy in the classroom comes from the teacher. For example, does the teacher stand by the door waiting for her students to enter, individually greeting each one? Or is she sitting behind her desk, grading papers, when the bell rings? Each action sends a message.

Tone: Tone is critical for an educator because a student will pick up on a teacher's tone and feel either safe or intimidated. It's important for a teacher to keep her tone soft and gentle, not loud, intimidating, or angry. Encourage students to find you accessible by using a gentle, nonthreatening voice.

Stress: Teachers need to use verbal and vocal stress to emphasize words and ideas, in order to help students understand which ideas are the most important, and the ones worth remembering. For instance, a teacher must speak clearly, and not too fast, so students can hear and take in what she says. Additionally, she may empha-size important key terms by repeating herself, by using a hand gesture, or by speaking in a louder tone. She may even remind her students to write down what she says when she discusses a particular term or concept. She may pause for effect before giving an answer to ensure listening, or even stop speaking entirely, asking a student to fill in the missing word. It's important not to overuse this strategy, so students will listen and respond when they hear the teacher emphasizing a particular idea.

Inflection: Inflection is a key element of conversation. When a voice goes up, the listener assumes the speaker is asking a question. When it goes down, the speaker is making a statement. Keep your inflection friendly but appropriate. When a story is exciting, sound excited! If a story is sad, sound sad. Students will learn how to speak appropriately from listening to others. Showing emotion through inflexion is a key communication technique.

Eye contact: Active listening includes eye contact, and a teacher should make consistent eye contact with his students as often as possible. If he models active listening techniques, his students will be likely to follow. It may even be necessary to get down to the child's level to create eye contact, but this act will make the child feel listened to, appreciated, and respected.

Facial expressions: A gentle facial expression is important when speaking with a child, especially when the teacher is frustrated. Keeping the face relaxed and even maintaining a slight smile can help a child be more communicative. If a teacher looks angry or scary, the child may not feel comfortable sharing her feelings. In a situation in which the teacher needs the child to change her behavior, the change will not happen if the child cannot trust the teacher. If her fear gets in the way of having a conversation, the student will not be able to change.

Personal space: It is important to teach students about personal space. Some stu-dents may not understand that peers and adults need a respectful amount of space when they are having a conversation. If a student is having trouble understanding the boundaries, a teacher can gently remind her to take a few steps backward to give the participants enough personal space to feel comfortable.

SKILL 7.2	Is aware of how culture and gender can affect communication

Being culturally aware and creating a culturally responsive classroom is key to gaining student respect. Gloria Ladson-Billings, who discusses the term culturally responsive, explains that this type of classroom is an environment where all students, regardless of culture or gender, feel comfortable, safe, and respected. The teacher needs to learn the cultural details of her students, celebrate them when possible, and quietly respect them all the time. For example, some students may avoid eye contact, and some students may refuse to partner with a child of the opposite gender. Some students may not be comfortable approaching an adult figure with a problem, and other students may not understand why it is necessary to raise a hand when they want to speak. All of these challenges can break down communication. A teacher needs to communicate with her students in a way they feel comfortable. So, do not require eye contact from a student who cannot give it. Do not require students to work with partners of the opposite gender if they have a cultural reason that prohibits or discourages it. These challenges can become more difficult when the teacher is of a different culture or gender from most of the students. It may take more time for the students to respect the teacher as an authority figure, but the teacher should not give up. Instead, the teacher should take an interest in their lives, activate their prior knowledge whenever possible, and invest in creating a culturally responsive classroom.

All of these details make for a challenging classroom. While the teacher wants to create a safe and nurturing environment, he must do so by respecting all the differences in his classroom.

SKILL 7.3 Knows how to use various communication tools to enrich the learning environment

SKILL 7.3.1 Audio and visual aids

Audio aids can be very useful, especially for children who are just learning to read. Often, teachers include a listening center in their independent learning centers. Students can listen to directions through headphones and follow them to complete a puzzle or a problem-solving activity; for example, "Color all the rectangles blue." In this case, the student would pause the recording and complete the task. The recording could resume with: "Next, circle all the circles." The student would pause the recording and complete the task.

Additionally, students can listen to recordings of books and follow along in the text with their finger, tracking the words as they go by. These exercises give students a chance to learn independently and have the scaffolding of the audio aid. Often, phonics and math computer games will have an audio component. Children can listen to an interesting voice give them directions as they complete the game. These audio aids can help keep student interest and provide children with an additional component to match a specific learning style.

where all students, regardless of culture or gender, feel comfortable, safe, and respected. The teacher needs to learn the cultural details of her students, celebrate them when possible, and quietly respect them all the time. For example, some students may avoid eye contact, and some students may refuse to partner with a child of the opposite gender. Some students may not be comfortable approaching an adult figure with a problem, and other students may not understand why it is necessary to raise a hand when they want to speak. All of these challenges can break down communication. A teacher needs to communicate with her students in a way they feel comfortable. So, do not require eye contact from a student who cannot give it. Do not require students to work with partners of the opposite gender if they have a cultural reason that prohibits or discourages it. These challenges can become more difficult when the teacher is of a different culture or gender from most of the students. It may take more time for the students to respect the teacher as an authority figure, but the teacher should not give up. Instead, the teacher should take an interest in their lives, activate their prior knowledge whenever possible, and invest in creating a culturally responsive classroom.

Visual aids are important for young learners and visual learners of all ages. Graphs, charts, illustrations, colorful posters, blocks, games, and manipulatives are all visual aids that will help a student understand a concept. Teachers should use these on a daily basis, especially when they are teaching a new concept. Allowing students to touch an object, see what it looks like, and discuss its qualities can bring an abstract idea to life. For example, when students are learning how to count money, they can play with pretend coins and dollar bills. Being able to see and handle the coins will help students visualize and remember which coin represents which amount of money.

| SKILL 7.3.2 | Text and digital resources |

| SKILL 7.3.3 | Internet and other computer-based tools |

Visual aids are important for young learners and visual learners of all ages. Graphs, charts, illustrations, colorful posters, blocks, games, and manipulatives are all visual aids that will help a student understand a concept. Teachers should use these on a daily basis, especially when they are teaching a new concept. Allowing students to touch an object, see what it looks like, and discuss its qualities can bring an abstract idea to life. For example, when students are learning how to count money, they can play with pretend coins and dollar bills. Being able to see and handle the coins will help students visualize and remember which coin represents which amount of money.

Technology is ubiquitous in today's classrooms, and it will most likely be a part of every day's lessons. Whether in centers, as part of remediation, or as part of student research, computer-based tools are an integral part of today's classrooms. Computer-based resources are often student directed, which gives students more autonomy over their learning. Most students enjoy working with technology and look forward to this part of their day. However, an educator should understand the boundaries of technology, what it should be used for, and how to effectively bring it into class objectives.

For example, it is inappropriate to allow students to freely explore the Internet. Not all information on the Internet is reliable or appropriate for students. Fortunately, schools have security firewalls preventing students from accessing inappropriate sites, and school curriculum includes instruction on how to use the Internet safely and effectively.

When using computers in centers, set the technology prior to students using that center. That way you are not wasting time with technology issues, and students can get started immediately on the task.

Computers are not the only technological resource available. SMART boards, tablets, and even cell phones are often available for student use. SMART boards are projector screens that can interact with a computer, making it easy for students to see teacher corrections, interact with an exercise, solve a math problem, or even move pieces around with their fingers. SMART boards are mostly used for large-group work or direct instruction.

In addition, tablets and phones can be used for research purposes, note taking, or organizing information. Some schools even have "bring your own device" (BYOD) policies, which allow students to use their own technological devices in permitted areas ("green zones") in school. Although this gives students many opportunities for student-directed learning and research, teachers must be vigilant about student safety. Additionally, it's important to use technology as a supplement to, not a replacement for, traditional curriculum.

SKILL Understands effective listening strategies.
7.4

SKILL Explains and provides examples of active listening strategies such
7.4.1 as attending to the speaker, restating key points, asking questions,
interpreting information, providing supportive feedback, and
being respectful

Active listening is a key part of the teacher/student relationship. If neither party is listening to the other, students will not reach their goals. Learning is fluid, and the teacher needs to use active listening skills to understand how students are feeling, what they are struggling with, and what role she needs to play.

Active listening includes making eye contact, using open body language, restating the speaker's points, and offering validation to what the speaker is feeling. However, it is also important to ask questions. For example, if a student is discussing her feelings about another student, the teacher can restate and ask a further question such as, "You feel angry with Javier because he didn't include you in his game. Did you ask if you could be included?" If the student says yes, the teacher knows that he needs to ask more questions about the relationship between the two students. If the student says no, the teacher can remind her that Javier may not have known she wanted to play, and next time she should ask to join in. Asking furthering questions and interpreting the answers can give the teacher a clearer idea of what happened so he can help the student choose the most effective course of action.

Having this type of conversation with a student is supportive and respectful. The teacher is validating the feelings of the student and asking more about the situation. It is not beneficial to accuse a student of a certain behavior. Even if a teacher is certain that a student has made a poor choice, asking respectful questions is a more supportive strategy. A teacher could say, "I saw that you and Joey were arguing. Do you want to tell me what happened?" This is more useful than saying, "Why did you hit Joey?" The student will have the responsibility to explain his actions in his words. If he does not bring up hitting, then the teacher can ask a leading question: "Did you use your hands to solve that conflict?" If Joey then admits to hitting, the teacher can say, "What could you have done differently? Can we think of a better choice for next time?"

Having these conversations with students helps them make their own decisions. Hopefully, they remember some of the alternative solutions discussed with the teacher.

> Active listening includes making eye contact, using open body language, restating the speaker's points, and offering validation to what the speaker is feeling.

DOMAIN III
ASSESSMENT

PERSONALIZED STUDY PLAN

PERSONALIZED STUDY PLAN

COMPETENCY 8
ASSESSMENT AND EVALUATION STRATEGIES

> **SKILL** **Understands the role of formal and informal assessment in informing**
> **8.1** **the instructional process**

> **SKILL** **Defines and provides uses and examples of formal and informal**
> **8.1.1** **assessment modes**

Assessments happen every day in the classroom. While some are formal, such as state assessments, progress testing, and teacher-prepared tests and quizzes, other assessments can be more spontaneous.

A summative assessment is a formal assessment that measures what a student has learned over a period of time. Summative assessments include tests, quizzes, state tests, and presentations. Formative assessment is an assessment that measures progress. It is not formal, and it can happen at any point. Formative assessments can be in the form of completing homework or worksheets, answering questions, filling out a graphic organizer, or talking to a teacher. Formative assessments are informal ways for the teacher to check in and see if her students are understanding the concept before she moves on. Formative assessments can also be peer evaluations, self-evaluations, journal entries, or any type of metacognitive activity. When a student is discussing his own learning process, he is assessing himself, which is an important part of creating intrinsic motivation and self-directed learning.

> **SKILL** **Explains a variety of ways the results of formal and informal**
> **8.1.2** **assessments are used to make educational decisions**

The major summative assessments, such as state testing, are used for school funding and for grouping students in classes for the following year. Students may be chosen for gifted or remedial programs based on testing. The results can be broken down into standards, and analysis can show which students struggle with which standards. If it is evident that many students are struggling with comprehension, there may be a remedial class for those students to help them improve their knowledge in that content area.

Informal assessments can be used on a daily basis to make small changes in instructional planning. For example, if a teacher does a quick comprehension check on a math strategy and notices that his students are still missing the concept, instead of moving forward with a new lesson he may reteach the first concept, doing another check at the end of his second instructional period. Additionally, short quizzes, homework assignments, and journal entries can measure a student where she is, without the pressure of her friends. When there are too many collaborative activities, it is easy to lose track of where each student is individually. Therefore, it is important to informally evaluate each child whenever possible. The teacher may reorganize groups, work with different students during centers, or send home more challenging work to some students. Informal assessments can give the teacher a glimpse into what his students need on a daily basis.

SKILL 8.2	Understands the distinctions among the different types of assessment

SKILL 8.2.1	Defines and provides uses and examples of formative, summative, and diagnostic assessment

Formative assessment: A formative assessment is often informal, and it shows where a student is at a moment in time. Formative assessments include quizzes, homework, group work, question and answer sessions, worksheets, and work completed at centers. A teacher can use formative assessments on a daily basis to measure how much her students have learned during her lesson.

Summative assessment: A summative assessment is often more formal, and it measures what a student has learned over a period of time. Summative assessments are often unit end tests, presentations, papers, or statewide exams. They measure mastery of knowledge: Are students ready to move on? Have they mastered the subject? Summative assessments are not used as often as formative assessments, and usually these are the exams that count toward student grades or even school funding.

Diagnostic assessment: A diagnostic assessment measures a particular student skill and will often give the teacher an idea of how one student compares to his peers. Often, students take diagnostic assessments for literacy or math skills at the beginning of a remediation program. However, a diagnostic assessment can also be used to measure knowledge prior to the start of a unit. A teacher may ask her class 10 questions about the Civil War, measuring to see if they have any background knowledge. A diagnostic assessment is a more formal tactic than creating a KWL chart, but it can have similar results, and because it is individual it can clearly show the teacher each student's knowledge base.

FORMATIVE ASSESSMENT: A formative assessment is often informal, and it shows where a student is at a moment in time.

SUMMARATIVE ASSESSMENT: A summative assessment is often more formal, and it measures what a student has learned over a period of time.

DIAGNOSTIC ASSESSMENT: A diagnostic assessment measures a particular student skill and will often give the teacher an idea of how one student compares to his peers.

SKILL 8.3 Knows how to create and select an appropriate assessment format to meet instructional objectives

SKILL 8.3.1 Knows how to create assessments in a variety of formats

Assessments can be formal or informal, traditional or nontraditional. If a teacher is collecting information on student knowledge, she is conducting an assessment. While some assessments, such as state testing, are mandatory, others are up to the teacher. Will the teacher tell her students about upcoming assessments? Or will some be a surprise? Will there be a standing quiz each Thursday on material learned, or will the quizzes be based on student progress? Teachers can choose to give written quizzes, tests, or essays, or they can evaluate students through oral discussion, cooperative learning, journaling, homework, or conference. Choosing a variety of formats when creating assessments is important because different assessments will allow students with various learning styles to succeed. While one student may be a horrible quiz taker, he may be an excellent presenter. Teachers should alternate assessment formats to help all students feel successful, discover student knowledge in a multitude of ways, and encourage creativity and growth in understanding new concepts.

SKILL 8.3.2 Is able to select an assessment format to meet a specific instructional objective

Before a teacher begins instruction, she will have a goal and objective. She will also know how she will measure her students' progress. Some formats will be more appropriate for certain skills than others. For example, giving an oral quiz may work well when drilling multiplication facts, but an oral quiz will not be helpful when measuring abstract concepts that require a written, well thought-out answer. Consider student stress level, difficulty in correcting, subjectivity versus objectivity, validity, and reliability when deciding which assessment format is the most appropriate.

SKILL 8.4 Knows how to select from a variety of assessment tools to evaluate student performance

Just like a teacher needs to teach for various learning styles, he needs to provide his students with multiple options for assessment. He may give his students a weekly quiz, but he should also use presentations, skits, interviews, board games, and papers as assessment tools. Children have varying strengths, so incorporating as many assessments as possible into the curriculum will ensure that each child feels comfortable with at least one or two.

> ### SKILL 8.4.1 Knows a variety of assessment tools, their uses, strengths, and limitations, such as rubrics, analytical checklists, scoring guides, anecdotal notes, continuums

Rubrics: A rubric is often given to a student prior to completing an open-ended, subjective assignment such as a paper, presentation, or project. It gives the students expectations for what the teacher will be looking for when she grades the assessment. There are often three or four categories, and next to each category a score of 1 to 4. One usually represents the lowest grade possible, while four represents the highest. Next to each number, the teacher writes a description of what type of work would receive that score. For example, in the category of creativity, a score of 1 may say, "Showed very little effort put into creating the prop for the presentation. Handwriting is messy and unclear." A score of 4 may say, "Excellent design in the prop. Use of multiple colors and clear, easy-to-read handwriting with correct facts stated on the prop. Creative choice of presentation." A student who receives a rubric prior to completing an assignment will know exactly how to succeed and can check her items off the list as she completes them. Giving students a rubric establishes guidelines when assigning a subjective project. Without a rubric, students will have very little knowledge of the expectations.

Analytical checklists/scoring guides: An analytical checklist or scoring guide is a type of rubric. It breaks down the project and gives each part of the project a specific point value. Some parts of the project can be weighted more heavily than others by giving them more points. For example, a teacher may place a higher priority on the thesis statement than on the reference page, because perhaps he has been focusing on writing thesis statements for the past few weeks. Unfortunately, a rubric like this can be intimidating to a student who wants perfect points for everything. Knowing exactly how many points each piece is worth can make creating an errorless project a daunting task.

Anecdotal notes: Teachers may take notes while watching students give a presentation or even before the actual assessment takes place. Perhaps the teacher was walking around and taking notes during collaborative learning to see which students were participating and which students were off task. The teacher can use these notes after the final presentation to grade group work, participation, or motivation to complete the task.

Continuums: An assessment continuum is a way to measure a student's progress in a domain or competency, such as reading or numerical understanding. The teacher categorizes the student according to many aspects of the skill, including the student's disposition toward the material, level of understanding, and ability to explain processes. Categories include Emerging, Developing, Applying, and Extending. As a student learns, he moves from Emerging (requires direct support), to Developing (requires guidance but not direct support), to Applying (requires minimal support), to Extending (requires no support and is able to connect the skill to real life).

To determine a student's progression on an assessment continuum, the teacher may start with a daily, formative assessment that checks for understanding. She may ask questions at the end of each class, do a journal check for understanding, or create a cooperative learning activity such as a think-pair-share. When she is further in the unit, she may give individual formative assignments, such as homework or comprehension worksheets. Next, she may do a class review game or study guide, prior to moving toward a summative assessment. Her summative assessments may begin with a test she created herself and then move on to district- and state-created exams.

Rubrics and Checklists: University of Texas, Austin (2009–2015).
http://www.utexas.edu/ugs/teaching/writing/grading/rubrics
Retrieved Jan. 23, 2015.

Continuum examples
British Columbia Education Teaching and Assessment Tools. http://www2.
gov.bc.ca/gov/DownloadAsset?assetId=80A0E21AB2F1485CA7CE1BD78
A41F5D0&filename=ol_continuum.pdf.
Retrieved Feb. 2, 2015.

Manitoba Education English Language Arts Developmental Reading Continuum.
http://www.edu.gov.mb.ca/k12/cur/ela/drc/drc_poster3.pdf.
Retrieved Feb. 2, 2015.

Choosing appropriate assessments
http://teachingcommons.cdl.edu/cdip/facultyteaching/
Choosingappropriateassessment.html
Retrieved Dec. 16, 2014.

SKILL 8.4.2 Is able to select an assessment tool appropriate for quantifying the results of a specific assessment

When determining which assessment tool to use, an educator first needs to decide if it will be quantitative or qualitative, and formative or summative. Will she give a formal quiz or observe students in collaborative groups? Once she has determined the assessment, she can decide how to quantify the results of that assessment. Sometimes, grading the assignment will be enough, especially if it is a quiz or test she has built herself. She then can find the mean, mode, and standard deviation if she likes and will have enough data to quantify the results. Sometimes, finding the mean will be sufficient to tell the practitioner what she needs to know about student achievement.

However, if the assessment is subjective, such as a paper or presentation, quantifying results is more difficult. The teacher can still find the mean of the scores, but because the scores themselves are more subjective, the mean is not as reliable. The teacher instead may look for understanding as his students move through the process or give the presentation.

Finally, if the assessment is on a large scale, such as a standardized test, the teacher may use Microsoft Excel to sort and then graph the data. He can break down the scores into standards, and he even can find descriptive statistics for each standard if he wants to be extremely detailed. The more detail the teacher finds, the more likely he will be to devise a plan for directed student improvement.

Pritchett, M. (2013). *Understanding assessment continuum as critical to student success.* http://navigator.compasslearning.com/featured/understanding-the-assessment-continuum-critical-to-student-success/
Retrieved Dec. 16, 2014.

Rubrics and Checklists
http://www.utexas.edu/ugs/teaching/writing/
grading/rubrics Retrieved Nov. 13, 2014.

SKILL 8.5 Understands the rationale behind and the uses of students' self and peer assessment

Professionals look at their own practice and reflect upon their strengths and weaknesses, and students can do the same. Self-assessments can begin the process of metacognition and self-reflection, and appropriately using a peer reflection can give a student an alternate point of view that can both reaffirm his strengths and gently point him in another direction if he is struggling with a concept. Peer reviews are especially useful in writing assignments because they can move the process forward in a way that is less intimidating than teacher reviews. Additionally, the teacher can use self and peer assessments as formative assessments as the class moves through a unit and prepares for the summative assessment at the end. The teacher can read the peers' feedback, comments, and rubrics as checkpoints for student understanding. Finally, research has shown that one of the best ways to internalize a concept is to teach it to someone else, and working through a peer assessment (working a rubric and then conferencing) can help the students document a concept learned in class.

SKILL 8.5.1 Defines and provides uses and examples of student self-assessment modes

Self-assessments can begin the process of metacognition and self-reflection, and appropriately using a peer reflection can give a student an alternate point of view that can both reaffirm his strengths and gently point him in another direction if he is struggling with a concept.

Portfolios also are examples of self-reflection.

Student self-assessment is used during and after projects or written assignments. Often teachers use a separate rubric for students to score their own performances after completing a group project, a written paper, or an oral presentation. This is a way to encourage students to measure their own performances and to understand their strengths and weaknesses and their participation in an assessment. Self-assessments can include rubrics, reflection logs, conferences with the teacher, or even setting goals prior to beginning a project or signing a contract for learning and then checking in with the teacher upon completion to see if the goals were met. Portfolios also are examples of self-reflection.

What do these self-assessments look like? A rubric is an assessment tool that breaks down the skills for an assignment into categories, each of which is given a number of possible points with descriptors on how to earn each set of points. The student receives points in each category based on how well he has completed each measured skill. For example, a rubric could measure how well a student wrote his introduction. The rubric may specify that to gain five points (perhaps the most for that category), the introduction needs to have an interesting attention-grabber, a clear topic sentence, a main idea, and a closing sentence. To gain three points, the written introduction may have some grammatical and organization flaws, and to gain two points, there may be severe lack of organization and many grammatical flaws. Sometimes the teacher will create the rubric and ask students to grade themselves after completing the exercise. At other times, the teacher will ask the students to create the rubrics in groups or with him as a scaffolded activity.

A reflection log may be more holistic than the detailed rubric. The teacher may give the students questions to answer on comprehension of the material, organization, and effort. This type of reflection encourages metacognition, because it invites students to think about how they learned, if they succeeded or felt challenged, and how much effort had to go into success. Were there specific aspects of the exercise that were easy for them? Were others more difficult? The teacher may ask students to write a journal entry articulating their experience with completing the project. The teacher may begin with guiding questions and then give students time to free write their answers.

Some teachers may prefer conferences, especially when teaching the writing process. In this setting, the teacher can go over the project with each student individually, and the child can share her frustrations and her successes and ask specific questions about her project. This type of self-assessment can be useful for a shy student who may feel uncomfortable asking questions in class. If a contract or goal setting was used, a conference is the perfect time to check in with the student and see if goals were met. Finally, a portfolio is a student's collection of work over a period of months. By reviewing their portfolios, students can see their growth and improvement, often with the teacher at a conference.

SKILL 8.5.2   Defines and provides uses and examples of peer assessment modes

A peer assessment is a formative assessment in which students give one another point values or comments based on how well they think a student participated in a project. Often peer assessments are used for group projects, presentations, or literature circles. While peers don't often score for grades, they may score effort or participation. Occasionally, peer review can be used to grade academic skill, but only if used correctly. Examples of peer assessment include peer reflections, rubrics, checklists, or anonymous grading.

When using a peer reflection, it is helpful to go over the expectations prior to giving students the checklist or rubric. Peer reflections often are formatted like self-reflections, except group members or partners will fill out the reflection for their group mates. It's important for students to understand the difference between constructive criticism and ineffective criticism.

Sometimes, a teacher will remove names from papers or quizzes, pass them out to the class, and ask students to write comments on the paper or grade the quiz. Teaching students to give feedback to other students will encourage empathy and reinforce knowledge learned in the unit.

SKILL 8.5.3   Explains the strengths and limitations of self and peer assessment modes

There are advantages and disadvantages to using self and peer assessments. Both can help students reinforce what they have learned by encouraging them to move slowly through the material, looking for mistakes as well as areas of strength. Additionally, peer assessments can help students learn from one another as they see how other students have handled similar questions. However, it is important to keep the environment safe and nurturing, or a peer assessment can easily become competitive; this is a limitation of using peer assessments. Additionally, students' self-worth can suffer if there is a noticeable difference in quality among students' papers.

SKILL 8.6 **Knows how to use a variety of assessment formats**

SKILL 8.6.1 **Describes and provides uses, strengths, and limitations of a variety of assessment formats such as essay, selected response, portfolio, conference, observation, performance**

Teachers choose different types of assessments depending on what they are trying to assess, how their students can show their knowledge, and why they are giving the assessment. Each type has strengths and weaknesses, which we will discuss in this section.

> *Essays, presentations, performance, and portfolios are all performance assessments.*

The first type of assessment is a performance assessment. Essays, presentations, performance, and portfolios are all performance assessments. An essay is a good way for a teacher to measure higher-level thinking or conceptual understanding. Often, an essay assignment will include questions that begin with why or how, or it may use words such as explain, describe, or analyze. The teacher also may be measuring how well a student can organize her thoughts and the student's grammatical skills. Essays can be effective because they measure a number of skills, not just the concept being studied. Often, teachers use essays as summative assessments, as take-home exams, or even as opportunities to practice the writing process, which also can include peer and self-assessment. However, there are some limitations to asking students to write essays. Grading an essay is very subjective, even if the teacher provides students with a detailed rubric. Additionally, some students may feel intimidated by writing an essay. They may have a hard time expressing their knowledge if they are overwhelmed by the grammar and organization needed to create a well-structured essay. Therefore, if a teacher just wants to measure factual knowledge, an essay is not the best choice. Other assessments are perfect for this purpose.

Portfolios are another type of performance assessment. Teachers often use portfolios in humanities classes such as language arts, history, art, or social sciences. Teachers can measure growth in writing, organization, or even handwriting. Portfolios also are excellent for self-assessment. Students can see their own growth and practice metacognitive skills as they discuss their progress with a teacher at conferences throughout the year. However, portfolios have limitations. They are excellent for measuring the process of learning, but they are not good choices to measure a moment in time. Because, by definition, a portfolio is a process-based assessment, it should be used as such.

Conferences, observations, and performances also are types of performance assessments. Conferences and observations often are used when a teacher wants to assess individual performance and have a chance to talk over the uniqueness of each child's progress in a private setting. These are also excellent in providing authentic learning experiences in which a student feels like she is part of the entire assessment process, not just a test-taker. When giving a presentation, for example, students decide which information to include and how to present it, and they may work with a group to decide the best methods. Students will field questions from classmates, and, by taking on that instructor role, will see the material from an alternate perspective. Unfortunately, these types of assessments have limitations. Grading is often subjective, even with clear rubrics, and in group projects, sometimes one student works harder than another. Additionally, it takes much longer to prepare a presentation, conference with many students, or keep track of multiple observations than it would to give a test.

Selected response assessments, which include multiple-choice, matching, or true/false questions, are an excellent way to measure factual knowledge and lower levels of Bloom's taxonomy. These are not performance assessments. Sometimes, questions are written to measure conceptual knowledge, but there are limitations to these types of questions, which we will cover shortly. Many state exams and standardized tests are written in a selected response format, so it is important for students to become comfortable with these types of tests. Often, teachers will use these as summative assessments at the end of a unit. Selected response can be used to measure knowledge in multiple subjects such as history, math, language arts, and science. Strengths of selected response questions include the ability to measure factual knowledge and to easily detect weaknesses and gaps in student knowledge. They also are easily gradable. However, they have limitations. Sometimes a teacher may include responses such as "none of the above," which can open up the answer to interpretation and make finding the answer much more difficult. This can make students question their knowledge. Additionally, it is difficult to measure conceptual knowledge. Although some questions may begin with how, why, or explain and give longer answers from which to choose, students' subjectivity can get in the way of choosing the right answer. Selected response questions also must be checked for reliability and validity to ensure they are appropriate for all students from varied sociocultural backgrounds.

> ### SKILL 8.6.2 Is able to select an assessment format appropriate to a specific educational context

How do you know which assessment format is appropriate for a specific educational context? You need to know what you are trying to find out, how many students you have, how much time you have, and what is required of you. For example, if you need to know how many students know their multiplication facts, a timed quiz is probably your best option. However, if you want to know how many students conceptualized the theme of *Othello*, it may be better to ask for an essay, a presentation, or even a conference. Some of these assessments will be difficult if you have a large group of students. For example, interviewing 25 students may take a week, and essay questions could take hours to grade.

Sometimes, assessment formats will be required. For example, state tests and most standardized tests are created in a selected response format, and there are rules governing how the exam must be given. Additionally, if there is a time crunch on receiving and analyzing data, a selected response assessment often is the best choice.

Finally, if possible, take into account the needs and ages of the students. Whereas some students may thrive in a situation in which they have to give presentations, others may prefer to quietly write an essay. Sometimes it is possible to allow students to choose how they would like to be assessed. Perhaps you could offer three alternatives: an essay, a presentation, or an exam. Students can choose the one that is the most comfortable for them.

COMPETENCY 9
ASSESSMENT TOOLS

> **SKILL** **Understands the types and purposes of standardized tests**
> **9.1**

The idea behind the word standardized is that every student takes an identical test (although the order of questions might differ, and the test will be adapted for those with extreme, documented learning disabilities), and the scores are standardized and documented through a norm reference. Often, these tests are state testing, which is given to each student in the spring term and given on a computer. However, the SAT, GRE, ACT, LSAT, MCAT, and PRAXIS are also standardized tests. These tests, taken when students are about to move into higher education or professional fields, measure readiness to learn as well as knowledge learned. By studying with this book, you are preparing yourself for a standardized test!

These tests often have easily scored multiple-choice questions, but they also can include short answer, true/false, and essay questions. Computers often score the multiple-choice questions, but when there are essays involved, two or more humans must use a rubric to score these and then average their scores.

These standardized tests often measure aptitude, achievement, or readiness. For example, the SAT, LSAT, and ACT are aptitude tests, as they measure conceptual abilities and ability to problem solve. The yearly standardized tests taken in school are achievement tests, as they measure specific skills that students have been practicing all year. Finally, readiness tests include the PRAXIS, because they measure a person's ability to move toward earning a certificate in teaching. Often, the raw score is translated into a standard score and percentile, so the test taker can measure her score against those of her peers.

> **SKILL** **Explains the uses of the different types of standardized tests, such**
> **9.1.1** **as achievement, aptitude, ability**

There are four major types of standardized tests. Standardized tests are often used to measure progress across a group of students; to create data that shows which students are ahead, with, or behind the average; and to develop strategies for teaching. The four types of standardized tests are as follows:

An aptitude test measures a person's ability to learn a certain skill. These tests can be given at any time, because they measure a person's innate ability in various skills. In contrast, an achievement test measures a person's achievement after learning specific skills. Achievement tests are given after a person has been given an opportunity to learn a certain set of skills.

An ability test (also called an intelligence test) measures a person's ability to reason, plan, solve problems, think abstractly, comprehend ideas and language, and learn. (http://psychology.ucdavis.edu/faculty_sites/sommerb/ sommerdemo/stantests/mental.htm). IQ tests and yearly state tests are examples of ability tests.

Standardized test
http://edglossary.org/standardized-test/
Retrieved Dec. 16, 2014.

Standardized tests: Mental ability.
http://psychology.ucdavis.edu/faculty_sites/sommerb/sommerdemo/ stantests/mental.htm Retrieved Dec. 12, 2014.

SKILL 9.1.2 **Recognizes the data provided by the different types of standardized tests**

What kind of data do standardized tests provide? The most obvious kind of data is student strengths and weaknesses. Because standardized test questions often are organized into academic standards, by examining the pattern of correct and

incorrect answer choices a teacher can tell where a student is struggling and where the student is succeeding. This type of data analysis can lead to better and more focused instruction.

However, other types of data are available from standardized tests. The first is demographic data, which can tell an analyst the types of students who attend a given school. Gender, ethnicity, special needs, and other characteristics are included on a standardized test. Often students fill out demographic questions prior to completing the test.

Finally, schools can use data from standardized tests for school improvement. After looking at a group of students' scores, analysts can tell if the majority of students are grasping a concept, can suggest areas of instructional focus, and can determine whether specific intervention programs at the school are effective. If the results of the test show that the majority of students do not understand a concept, administrators can put into place programs that will help overall academic improvement.

SKILL 9.2 Understands the distinction between norm-referenced and criterion-referenced scoring

SKILL 9.2.1 Explains the uses of norm-referenced and criterion-referenced tests

Educators give norm-referenced and criterion-referenced assessments for different purposes. **A criterion-referenced test is an assessment given with the purpose of measuring individual students' skills or knowledge.** These types of tests measure specific skills or knowledge learned in a unit. What do students know before instruction begins? What have they learned at the end of the unit? Teachers or coaches create the questions for these tests to measure what has gone on recently in the classroom.

In contrast, **a norm-referenced test is an assessment given to measure students' knowledge when compared to other students who are in their same grade level or who are their same age.** Often, norm-referenced tests are standardized tests or state tests that measure state standards. In contrast to criterion-referenced tests, curriculum experts create questions for norm-referenced tests with the goal of measuring what children have learned over a long period of time. Norm-referenced tests measure skills that are conceptual and not necessarily representative of what students learned in school last month.

SKILL 9.2.2 Explains data provided by a norm-referenced and a criterion-referenced test

What type of data do different types of assessments provide? In a criterion-referenced assessment, the data given is for each individual student who took the test. What did each student learn? Each student's score may be assigned a grade, and students' work can be compared according to these grades. For example, a "C" grade traditionally is considered average, whereas an "A" grade is considered exceptional. The score often is expressed as out of 100 points; for example, an 80% or a 65%. The goal is for most students to succeed, so the teacher knows he has done a good job relating the material. If many students fail, the teacher may go back and reteach the concepts.

A norm-referenced test provides different data. Children are measured against other children who are at the same grade level, so their score is in comparison to others. Scores are normally given in percentiles, but also often on grade-level equivalent. We will talk more about scoring terminology in the next section.

Unlike criterion-referenced tests, in which students' scores are based only on their individual performance, scores on norm-referenced tests indicate where a student stands in relation to other students.

> Huitt, W. (1996). Measurement and evaluation: Criterion- versus norm-referenced testing. *Educational Psychology Interactive.* Valdosta, GA: Valdosta State University. Retrieved Dec. 14, 2014, from http://www.edpsycinteractive.org/topics/measeval/crnmref.html.

SKILL 9.3 Understands terminology related to testing and scoring

A teacher can't score a test or analyze the data from it unless she knows what she's looking for and what to do with the information once she finds it. The following is a description of the most basic testing and scoring terms.

SKILL 9.3.1 Defines and explains terms related to testing and scoring, such as validity; reliability; raw score; scaled score; percentile; standard deviation; mean; mode; and median; grade-equivalent scores; age-equivalent scores

Validity: Does the test measure what it intends to measure? Can the intended audience understand it? Often, before a test is given, it will be given to a comparable audience to measure if the assessment is clear, focused, and easy to understand.

Reliability: Are the results of the assessment consistent? Are they stable? Were they repeated when used on a similar demographic? Sometimes a test will be given more than once to the same group to determine consistencies in scores and repeated results.

Raw Score: A raw score is a student's basic score. How many questions did he get right? How many were there total? For instance, if he got 10 out of 12 correct, his raw score would be 10/12.

Scaled Score: Often, especially in a standardized test, raw scores are converted into scaled scores to make them easier to compare across students.

Percentile: When rounded to 100, what is the percent of the score? For example, a student who scored 65 out of 70 would receive a 93%.

The next four terms are all part of descriptive statistics, or measures of central tendency. Each of these terms relies on the center score to determine other patterns in the data.

Standard Deviation: The standard deviation measures how spread out the data is. For example, if all of the students in the class scored close to the mean score of 85, the standard deviation is small; the data will not be very spread out. However, if the mean score is 85, and some students scored close to 100 while others scored as low as 60, the data will be very spread out and the standard deviation will be large. It's important to note that sometimes there will be outliers, or data points that are far outside the standard deviation. If there are only one or two outliers, they often are not taken into account.

Mean: The mean is the average score. To find the mean or the average, add all of the scores and then divide them by the number of participants.

Mode: The mode is the number that occurs most often in a data set. For example, if there are 30 students taking a test, and 15 score a 75, 10 score a 95, and 5 score a 92, 75 is the mode because it is the number that occurs the most frequently.

Median: The median is the middle score. If there is an odd number of scores, take the middle score. If there is an even number of scores, average the middle two to find the middle score.

Grade-Equivalent Score: This type of measurement compares a student's score with those of other students in various grades. The score is given as a grade level, which shows whether the student is at, above, or below his current grade level.

Age-Equivalent Score: This measurement is the same as grade-equivalent score but compares ages rather than grades.

SKILL 9.4 | **Understands the distinction between holistic and analytical scoring**

SKILL 9.4.1 | **Describes holistic scoring and analytical scoring**

Holistic scoring is determined by looking at the overall idea behind the assessment, not specific details. For example, a teacher who is giving an essay a holistic score will not give the student's grammar or spelling a separate score. All the student's successes and errors will go into creating one score for the entire work. Before a teacher uses holistic scoring, he must inform his students of how they will receive the grade. The teacher must make it clear what he is looking for and how he will be grading the paper.

In contrast, **analytic scoring is when each section of the assessment is broken down into categories, which are each given their own score.** For example, a teacher may grade for grammar, organization, spelling, and transitions—all separately. This method is often viewed as more reliable because each skill is examined individually.

Holistic vs. analytic scoring of writing
https://facultystaff.richmond.edu/~rterry/Middlebury/holistic.htm
Retrieved Dec. 14, 2014.

| SKILL 9.4.2 | Identifies an educational context for each |

When is it appropriate to use holistic scoring, and when is it better to use analytical scoring? It depends on context, time, and the age of the students. Holistic scoring is much faster, so if there is a time crunch, holistic scoring will give the teacher an idea of where each student is in the skill but will not take hours of painstaking grading. Additionally, younger students may feel overwhelmed by multiple categories and may perform better when the scoring is holistic. However, if the teacher is looking for particular growth and attention to certain skills, such as grammar or transition words, analytic scoring is the better choice. This type of scoring is especially useful if the teacher has just completed a unit on a particular skill and wants to measure how well students can use it in writing an essay.

| SKILL 9.5 | Knows how to interpret assessment results and communicate the meaning of those results to students, parents/caregivers, and school personnel |

Once a teacher has received assessment data and has calculated the descriptive statistics, what is next? The teacher must share that information with various stakeholders, including students, parents, and often administrators. Administrators may see the data before the teachers, but the teachers will have the opportunity to analyze the data and evaluate where their students fall in each skill set.

The most important stakeholder is the student. Before any big exam—even months before—the teacher should sit down with the student and decide on goals. The teacher should already be aware, from prior assessments, what the child needs to be working on. The teacher can conference with the student and discuss the goals the student would like to attain before and during the exam. After the teacher has analyzed the student's score, the teacher can speak with the student privately, discussing whether he reached his academic goals, which skills he found easy, and which are still challenging and need more work. These conferences create self-awareness and practice metacognitive skills, which will be crucial to a student's ability to be intrinsically motivated.

Some young students may not be ready for such an intense discussion. In this case, the teacher can holistically discuss the scores and casually talk about what can be improved.

The next stakeholder is the parents or caregivers. Often, the school will send out a detailed report of individual student scores, comparing them to the average. Parents can read the report and understand where their child falls in comparison to other students, based on percentiles. However, sometimes these reports can be difficult to understand. The teacher may choose to send out a more informal memo to the parents, explaining each child's strengths and challenges. This would also be a great place to discuss goals the child met and areas that need more practice. Additionally, if the child qualifies for any remedial services offered by the school (different from special education and based solely on test scores), the teacher can alert the parent to the programs in which the child will have the opportunity to participate.

Finally, school personnel are important stakeholders. School funding and grants can be given or taken away based on standardized test scores, so administrators are very interested in how students perform. Often, they will create spreadsheets that explore inferential statistics and determine what students need for improvement. What types of skills are students struggling with? What type of professional development will need to be created to help teachers learn what they need to teach? How can administrators support teachers as they move through these challenges? Administrators will be looking at questions like these as they analyze and evaluate standardized data.

SKILL 9.5.1 Understands what scores and testing data indicate about a student's ability, aptitude, or performance

Remember that aptitude, ability, and performance are different. A student's ability to answer questions on certain skills can be measured through standardized tests. For example, if there are 12 questions on main idea, and the student gets 10 correct, it is safe to assume that the student understands the concept of "main idea." However, getting questions wrong doesn't mean the student doesn't have the ability to succeed in a skill. Perhaps the student is a bad test-taker or synthesizes information in a different way. It's important to remember this when making assumptions about a student.

Aptitude tests can be used for predictions, for example, gauging how well a student will do in verbal or math skills as she gets older. An aptitude assessment is not about what the student has recently learned, but about how she has synthesized what she already knows. Aptitude tests also can compare students across categories to see which students are performing at a higher level and which are at a lower level. Additionally, because aptitude tests measure ability, special education teachers can see where their students are naturally successful and how they can use these strengths to help them learn through their challenges. After analyzing data from an aptitude exam, a teacher can adjust his instruction based on needs. Additionally, a school will be able to choose coursework and advanced courses based on the average aptitude of the student population.

Performance on a test is equal to the basic score. How did the child do? Did she perform well on the exam compared to her past scores and/or compared to her peers? Are her scores improving, or did they go down? Some students are natural test-takers, and others are not. This needs to be taken into account when measuring student performance on any assessment, especially high-stakes, high-stress state testing.

Macklem, Gayle L. (1990). Measuring aptitude. *Practical Assessment, Research & Evaluation,* 2(5). Retrieved Dec. 14, 2014 from http://PAREonline.net/getvn.asp?v=2&n=5.

> ### SKILL 9.5.2 Is able to explain results of assessments using language appropriate for the audience

When speaking to various stakeholders about the results of assessments, take into account the age, background, interest, and priorities of the stakeholder. Although you will not discuss standard deviation with a fifth grader, you may point out the student's percentile and grade equivalent score so he can understand where he falls in relation to peers.

Alternatively, when speaking with parents, you may create graphs that show the norm references and also show the student's progress throughout the year. Bar graphs or pie charts can be helpful. Parents or caregivers may not understand the gravity of the assessment, so giving them a short summary of the purpose and methods of the test prior to showing the results can be helpful.

Finally, administrators or peers may want a detailed report of student scores, including the standards on which a student succeeded and those that were challenging. To do this, a teacher may need to analyze each question, connect it to a standard, and then chart the results. This type of data analysis is time consuming, but it will give the educators the most detailed picture of what the students need for improvement.

DOMAIN IV
PROFESSIONAL DEVELOPMENT, LEADERSHIP, AND COMMMUNITY

PERSONALIZED STUDY PLAN

KNOWN MATERIAL/ SKIP IT

PAGE	COMPETENCY AND SKILL	
126	**10.1: Is aware of a variety of professional development practices and resources, such as professional literature, professional associations, workshops, conferences, learning communities, graduate courses, independent research, internships, mentors, study groups**	☐
128	**10.2: Understands the implications of research, views, ideas, and debates on teaching practices**	☐
	10.2.1: Knows resources for accessing research, views, and debates on teaching practices	☐
	10.2.2: Interprets data, results, and conclusions from research on teaching practices	
	10.2.3: Is able to relate data, results and conclusions from research and/or views, ideas, and debates to a variety of educational situations	☐
130	**10.3: Recognizes the role of reflective practice for professional growth**	☐
	10.3.1: Defines the purposes of reflective practice	☐
	10.3.2: Knows a variety of activities that support reflective practice, such as reflective journal, self and peer assessment, incidental analysis, portfolio, peer observation, critical friend	☐
132	**10.4: Is aware of school support personnel who assist students, teachers, and families, such as guidance counselors; IEP team members; special education teachers; speech, physical, and occupational therapists; library media specialists; teachers of the gifted and talented; para educators**	☐
134	**10.5: Understands the role of teachers and schools as educational leaders in the greater community**	☐
	10.5.1: Role of teachers in shaping and advocating for the profession	☐
	10.5.2: Perceptions of teachers	☐
	10.5.3: Partnerships with parents and family members	☐
	10.5.4: Partnerships with the community	☐
136	**10.6: Knows basic strategies for developing collaborative relationships with colleagues, administrators, other school personnel, parents/caregivers, and the community to support the educational process**	☐

PERSONALIZED STUDY PLAN

KNOWN MATERIAL/ SKIP IT

PAGE	COMPETENCY AND SKILL	
	10.6.1: Knows the elements of successful collaboration, such as developing an action plan, identifying the stakeholders, identifying the purpose of the collaboration, supporting effective communication, seeking support	☐
137	**10.7: Understands the implications of major legislation and court decisions relating to students and teachers, such as equal access, privacy and confidentiality, First Amendment issues, intellectual freedom, mandated reporting of child neglect/ abuse, due process, liability, licensing, tenure, copyright**	☐

COMPETENCY 10

> **SKILL 10.1** Is aware of a variety of professional development practices and resources, such as professional literature, professional associations, workshops, conferences, learning communities, graduate courses, independent research, internships, mentors, study groups

Professional development should be ongoing, intensive, and relevant to the teacher. In addition, teachers should be given multiple opportunities to practice their new skills. Often, professional development is a one-time workshop, which doesn't provide an opportunity for later practice or reflection. When this is the case, there is very little improvement in practice.

Professional development should be ongoing, intensive, and relevant to the teacher. In addition, teachers should be given multiple opportunities to practice their new skills. Often, professional development is a one-time workshop, which doesn't provide an opportunity for later practice or reflection. When this is the case, there is very little improvement in practice. However, teachers should not rely on administrators to provide opportunities for improvement. There are many ways to continually improve practice independently.

Professional Literature: There are many professional journals and books on the practice available to the educator. Some are free online, others require subscriptions, and others are available in bookstores or given at workshops. For example, the National Council of Teacher Educators is a peer-reviewed journal that covers everything from classroom strategies to new ideas in education. This journal is available at http://www.ncte.org/journals. Subscribing to journals such as this can help teachers stay abreast of the newest research and keep their practice current.

Professional Associations: Some teachers, especially those who work in public schools, will be asked to join a union. The goals of union membership include protecting teachers from unfair treatment, setting boundaries on their hours, and defining pay scales and overtime compensation. Unions can be useful, but they also can put teachers in positions in which they are asked to agree with the union for the greater good, which can cause stress.

Workshops/Conferences/Learning Communities: Often, a school will offer various mandatory professional development seminars throughout the year that are relevant to the school as a whole. However, a teacher may want to attend a workshop or conference outside school that is particular to his subject matter or to a challenge that he faces. Professional development, according to Linda Darling-Hammond, should be ongoing and relevant, and sometimes a teacher will have to seek out an opportunity that is the most relevant to his needs.

Sometimes, the school will be able to pay for these outside opportunities (some of them are even out of state) if they align with the school's needs. Often, the school may contribute some money toward the workshop and cover the cost of a substitute for the teacher, and the teacher will be responsible for covering the rest of the cost. These workshops and conferences can expose educators to new technologies, new strategies, and new management skills, presented by passionate individuals. Additionally, workshops or conferences often can count toward learning units necessary for renewing a teaching license.

Graduate Courses: A teacher may choose to take graduate courses, either toward a higher degree or because the teacher wants to learn more about a certain aspect of her profession. Generally, if a teacher obtains a higher degree, she will earn a higher salary. Graduate courses may be done online, at night, or sometimes on the weekends, and they often can count toward renewing a professional teaching license with the state. Because a teacher will have to renew his license every few years, graduate coursework is an excellent way to continue to stay current and also earn credits for the state.

Independent Research: A teacher may identify a problem in her classroom or within her team and want to find a solution. The teacher may conduct independent research or action research to find a practical solution that she can implement. Conducting action research can be as simple or as complicated as necessary to reach a solution. For example, if a teacher wants to find out if her students will learn better in a center-focused environment, she may devise a series of centers over a couple of weeks and then give her students a summative assessment to measure the knowledge they have been practicing. If scores are substantially higher than previous scores, which are based on a higher level of direct instruction, she can assume that her center-focused classroom is helpful.

Larger action research projects may include complicated subjects such as obtaining a higher level of parental involvement or finding strategies to motivate students who have behavior issues in class. These types of independent research projects may take longer to research, identify, and implement solutions and to measure and evaluate the results.

Internships: New teachers usually are required to complete one or two internships, called student teaching, to complete their degree. In these internships, a student teacher will observe a more experienced teacher, begin some teaching, and reflect upon the challenges he will face. Often, the more experienced teacher will become a mentor to the student teacher.

As a teacher goes through his career, he may have the opportunity to take part in different types of internships. He may go back to school to obtain a higher degree, and completing an internship will be a major component of that degree plan. In these internships, because the teacher is more experienced, he may be able to work with administrators, develop an action research project, and write more complicated reflections as he learns about the world beyond the classroom. All of these opportunities can help the teacher become a more efficient and successful educator.

Mentors: Mentors can be formal or informal. Often, administrators will assign formal mentors to new teachers to coach them through the difficulties of the first year or two. The mentor may earn a stipend for meeting with the teacher, observing her, providing feedback on classroom management and practice, and giving her ideas for lesson planning or strategies for difficult students. Informal mentors may be peers who take an interest in a new teacher to the profession or district and offer help on curriculum, behavior management, and strategies. Informal mentors can be very useful to new teachers, because they can help a new hire navigate the culture of the students, which would be extremely difficult without any aid.

Study Groups: A teacher study group is a type of professional development. It is a type of professional learning community (PLC) in which teachers share experiences. It is a collaborative and communicative effort in which personal experiences, self-reflections, and background knowledge come together to enhance all participants' teaching. To be successful, the study group must respect the teachers' time, have established goals, and match the needs of the educators. Often there will be a "coach," or leader of the study group who facilitates reaching the group's goals, directs conversation, and keeps the participants on task.

Walpole, S. (2008). http://www.literacycoachingonline.org/briefs/ StudyGroupsBrief.pdf. Retrieved Dec. 15, 2014.

> **SKILL 10.2** Understands the implications of research, views, ideas, and debates on teaching practices

> **SKILL 10.2.1** Knows resources for accessing research, views, ideas, and debates on teaching practices

A teacher should always be learning. At every point in the teacher's career, he should be intrinsically motivated to find new strategies for teaching and learning. But what resources are available to do this? Journals are ubiquitous, and they are available online or by hard-copy subscription. Often, joining a union will give a teacher access to newsletters or magazines. Additionally, taking graduate courses, working with a mentor, reading books, and speaking with peers can give the practitioner alternative views and advice on teaching practices. Often, a teacher mentor will give the teacher mentee reading material that can help the mentee adjust to a new environment.

SKILL 10.2.2 Interprets data, results, and conclusions from research on teaching practices

Data and results from standardized test scores, action research, or informal assessments and research need to be used effectively, or the research is wasted. Analyze data by breaking down questions into standards. Find the percentage of success of each standard. What percentage of students answered questions about main ideas correctly? What percentage of students answered questions about metaphorical language correctly? Once analysis is completed, the teacher needs to apply the analysis. The primary way to do this is to alter instructional practices to address areas in which students struggle, often by presenting the difficult concepts in a different way.

SKILL 10.2.3 Is able to relate data, results, and conclusions from research and/or views, ideas, and debates to a variety of educational situations

Educational situations are not limited to the classroom. Professional learning communities (PLCs), mentor/mentee conversations, and formal and informal observations are all educational situations that can be altered based on data, results, and conclusions from research. There are three types of research: quantitative, qualitative, and mixed methods. Although there are many types of quantitative and qualitative methods, we will cover the basics in this section.

A quantitative study is a study in which a researcher collects factual information—often gleaned from surveys, assessments, or mathematical data collection—and synthesizes it, creating descriptive and inferential statistics to measure a difference, a growth, or the effectiveness of an intervention. A qualitative study is a study that is more story-oriented; often, the researcher collects data through interviews, observations, or a combination of both. The data is then categorized and coded, and the researcher looks for themes in the conversations, which can then be used to create an answer to the hypothesis and sometimes a solution, if the situation is problem-based. It has been noted in research that the best type of inquiry is mixed methods; that is, it combines qualitative and quantitative methods to give the researcher the most well-rounded picture of the situation.

Once a researcher has analyzed the data and determined the results, the researcher can implement these results in her classroom. Implementation may take the form of a new instructional practice, a different method of classroom management, a new program, a PLC or professional development opportunity, and so on. However, if no change is made, the research is not useful or effective.

SKILL 10.3 Recognizes the role of reflective practice for professional growth

REFLECTION: Reflection is a metacognitive activity through which an educator discovers what he knows, what he is learning, how he is learning it, and what he is struggling with.

There is no growth without change, and in order to create change, there must be reflection. Reflection is a metacognitive activity through which an educator discovers what he knows, what he is learning, how he is learning it, and what he is struggling with. It is not always individual; it also can happen in professional learning communities. Examples of reflective practice include, but are not limited to, journals, incident reports, observation, mentor visits, discussions with peers, and attendance at professional workshops. The purpose of reflection is to become a better educator: to look at the objectives of the day, the response of the students and of the educator, the connections made with other experiences, and any improvements that could be made.

> (2007). A spotlight on reflective practice. http://www.education.vic.gov.au/
> Documents/childhood/professionals/support/spotref.pdf
> Retrieved Dec. 17, 2014.

SKILL 10.3.1 Defines the purposes of reflective practice

The purpose of reflective practice for an educator is to understand why she acts the way she does and why she chooses the instructional and behavioral methods that she does. Being metacognitive and critical about the practice will improve a teacher's attitude toward challenges, and in turn, her students' success. Learning, as discussed by sociocultural theorists, comes from experience. Therefore, if a teacher documents and reflects on his experience, he is more likely to keep what was successful and make a change to avoid the situations that were not successful in the future. Sometimes, reflective practice is not just documenting events, but also talking to stakeholders, defining a problem within the school, and searching for a solution.

SKILL 10.3.2 Knows a variety of activities that support reflective practice such as reflective journal, self and peer assessment, incident analysis, portfolio, peer observation, critical friend

Teachers should be reflective in their practice, and, ideally, this reflection should be ongoing and done with peers and superiors for teachers to get a full idea of the strengths and challenges of their practice. Fortunately, there are many ways to be reflective. Not all of these need to be used, but choosing one or two that match the needs of the educator can be an excellent way of keeping a current practice that is based in new research and is collaborative and successful.

Reflective Journal: A reflective journal can be private—where the teacher writes down events and later processes how she acted and what she could have done differently—or they can be shared with a team or an administrator. Sometimes, journals may be required of new teachers, especially if they are given a mentor. The mentor can read and respond to the journal and, in this way, keep the new teacher from feeling overwhelmed. Sometimes, there may be guided questions to answer in the journal; other times, the practitioner will be encouraged to free-write about a specific event or situation. Processing through writing also can be cathartic for teachers, especially after a particularly difficult—even traumatic—situation.

Self and Peer Assessment: These tools often are used in the classroom for students, and they have similar goals when used for educators. Teachers may be asked or required to fill out self-assessment forms, which may ask for demographic information about them and their students and for information about their practice, knowledge, and instructional strategies. Often, these are used prior to a formal observation or peer assessment with a fellow teacher or administrator. The teacher can measure her own practice and then discuss similarities with her peers. Self-reflections are excellent metacognitive tools because they encourage analysis of practice.

Peer assessments have similar goals, but they are less private. Often, one teacher will observe another and then fill out a predetermined form that could be in a rubric style, Likert scale, or open-ended questions. Peer assessments can be about classroom practice, lesson planning, or even working with other team members. The questions on the assessment will reflect the goal. Often, following the assessment, the two professionals can sit down together and discuss the results, talking about strengths and devising strategies to work on improvements. This type of assessment, when used effectively, can improve practice. To be effective, however, the environment must be one of trust; no one wants to feel unjustly criticized.

Incident Analysis: An incident analysis is when a teacher writes about and reflects upon a particular incident that stood out in his mind. This can be something successful or something that the teacher felt was a failure or challenge. The teacher may follow a specific guide in answering questions about the incident, such as documenting what happened, why, what could have been done differently, and how this will affect future practice. Next, the teacher will discuss these reflections with his peers and receive feedback about the experience. The idea is that after the incident analysis the teacher has a strategy for the next time something similar occurs.

Portfolio: A portfolio is a long-term project in which a teacher keeps paperwork, records, and assessments in a folder for months or even years. Often, a teacher will set goals for herself and use the artifacts in the portfolio to see if she has reached her goals. Sometimes, if the teacher is trying to reach a particular student goal, he may include copies of student work. Portfolios are kept private between the teacher and sometimes his mentor or administrator, so including anonymous student work is acceptable.

Peer Observation: Often, self and peer assessments will go with peer observations, but sometimes an observation is just a teaching tool. Sometimes peer observations can be casual, and other times they can be more formal. Sometimes a teacher may ask a peer to observe a particular student, group, or lesson for suggestions on how to improve. Perhaps the teacher struggles with classroom management, but knows that her more experienced peer has an excellent system. The newer teacher can observe the more experienced one to learn about that teacher's strategies, and then the experienced teacher can observe the newer one and teach her when and how to apply these strategies. An administrator may do a more formal observation, which may include goal setting, observation forms, and conferences. Both formal and informal observations can help improve practice and can encourage metacognitive skills. However, as stated above, a safe environment is key; to trust the observer, take the observer seriously, and then commit to improvement, the teacher will need to feel respected throughout the process.

Critical Friend: A critical friend can be a casual observer who may be in the same field but may not work in the same setting. Perhaps the practitioner calls on the critical friend for support, asks for advice, or explains a particular situation with which he is struggling. The outside perspective can often be useful in creating a solution or seeing the problem from a different perspective.

A teacher is not alone in the classroom. The teacher is not solely responsible for the success of his students. There are many supporting roles in a school that can be excellent resources for the classroom teacher, if he knows how to use each one.

SKILL 10.4	Is aware of school support personnel who assist students, teachers, and families, such as guidance counselors; IEP team members; special education teachers; speech, physical, and occupational therapists; library media specialists; teachers of the gifted and talented; para educators

Guidance Counselors: Guidance counselors teach social skills classes in the elementary grades, help with student behavior in all grades, and are available for college counseling and scheduling issues for high school. They are trained in interpersonal skills, particularly in working with students who struggle socially, academically, and even in their home life, and they can help teachers create plans to help students who are struggling in the classroom. Guidance counselors may meet with struggling students on a regular basis to work on social skills and behaviors.

IEP team members: IEP team members are a wonderful resource. Often, they include a special education teacher, a classroom teacher, a speech or occupational therapist (depending on what services the child needs), an administrator, and a parent or caregiver. All of these team members know the child in a different capacity and have distinctive training in their chosen field. Often in IEP meetings, strategies for learning will be discussed and written down so that all who are working with the student can implement the same concepts. When a teacher sits in on an IEP meeting, the teacher will learn how to help the student, what the student's requirements are for accommodations, and how the student learns best. Again, this is a situation in which the teacher can communicate with the student's parents or caregivers to discuss their perspective—key to student success.

Special Education Teachers: Special education teachers are specifically trained to work with struggling students. Some do not have their own classroom, but team-teach inclusion classes with regular education teachers. Others teach small groups throughout the day. Their strengths are in differentiated instruction, attending and providing input during IEP meetings, writing IEPs, teaching by using multiple intelligences, and communicating with parents and caregivers. Often, special education teachers have ideas for success that the classroom teacher may not have implemented. Some of these strategies can be small but crucial, such as moving an inattentive student to the front of the class, and others can be more dramatic, like creating a homework organization plan for a student struggling with attention issues.

Speech, Physical, and Occupational Therapists: These therapists often are employed by the district but move around from school to school. It is rare that a therapist will work for only one school. Most often, children are placed with these specialists because of a requirement in their IEP. Students are pulled out of their regular classroom setting to see the therapist a few times a week. A speech therapist will work on speaking clearly with the child; a physical therapist works on helping a student through an injury or disability, which may include tissue or structural challenges. An occupational therapist may work with a student on self-regulatory skills to manage sensory issues, handwriting, and other day-to-day skills. For some students who are severely disabled, an occupational therapist may help them learn to hold a fork, feed themselves, or use the bathroom.

Library Media Specialists: A library media specialist may give classes on the library, Internet safety, and how to use the Internet for research purposes. Classes may attend the media specialist's short seminars throughout the school year to learn how to do research. The media specialist provides the lesson plan and strategies appropriate for the grade level. Sometimes children will learn how to use the library itself; other times, they will focus on how to use the available technology.

Teachers of the Gifted and Talented: Often, depending on the aptitude of the students, there are multiple gifted and talented classes in a school building, each of which has its own gifted and talented teachers. These teachers have special training in the needs of gifted and talented children, which can be unique. Often, these students move quickly through academics but can be highly sensitive and emotionally needy. These teachers can be excellent resources in challenging students who need more advanced material and in working with students who have complex emotional needs.

Para Educators: A para educator is a teaching assistant. Sometimes, para educators have a bachelor degree, but sometimes they do not. Often, they receive little or no training before beginning to work in the classroom. Some teachers ask para educators to help with managing student behavior, preparing lessons, grading papers, or teaching/managing small groups or centers. Keep in mind that it is not useful to put the neediest children in a small group with just the para educator, who does not necessarily have the appropriate training and may feel overwhelmed by the academic and social needs of the children. It is a better strategy to invite a para educator to manage a center and to give him tools to be an effective assistant teacher.

SKILL 10.5	Understands the role of teachers and schools as educational leaders in the greater community

SKILL 10.5.1	Role of teachers in shaping and advocating for the profession

A teacher sets the tone for the classroom, and teachers as a whole set the tone for how society perceives them. Therefore, it's important for teachers to respect their own profession and to advocate for themselves. What do teachers need to be successful? What sort of professional development needs to be available to make teachers more prepared to handle their particular classroom context? Advising administration on their needs, setting high expectations for themselves, and being aware of current legislation that affects their profession is key to their participation in shaping the profession. Letters to the Department of Education or state legislators may be effective in deciding policy, when they are sent in large groups. Often, unions can be helpful in mobilizing a large group of educators to gain the attention of legislators.

SKILL 10.5.2	Perceptions of teachers

How do teachers perceive their job? Do they believe they are important problem solvers, or do they believe they don't have much say in the school's curriculum or maintenance? How do they view their students? Some may have biased perceptions of particular populations, due to either negative experiences that they have generalized or lack of education. Others may favor one population over another, due to fears or stereotyping. Biased perceptions of students can affect the students' success, since children will pick up on favoritism.

Teachers should see themselves as agents of social change. Their opinions and experiences can affect the entire field of education, so they must be aware of this influence in classroom conversations, conversations with peers, and discussions with administrators or during professional conferences. It is important for teachers to see their job as critical not only to the development of today's youth, but also to the development of society as a whole. Teaching is not just educating students on the standards—it is showing children the values of their society and building a community. Educators have various priorities in the classroom. Whereas some believe that academics should be the priority, others believe that teaching children to be community leaders should be the priority. Whatever a teacher's perception of her job, she can prioritize this ideal into her lessons.

SKILL 10.5.3 Partnerships with parents and family members

Partnerships with families are crucial to student success. Research has consistently shown that the more involved families are, the more motivated children are to succeed and the more they do succeed. But creating these partnerships can be challenging. Parents may want to be involved but may find it difficult. Perhaps they work full time, speak another language, or have multiple children who need lots of attention. While some parents will always volunteer to be room parent, chaperone field trips, and be a member of the PTA, others will not because they don't want to or cannot. It is important to keep in mind that formal participation is not the only option. At the beginning of the year, the teacher can send out a short survey asking parents for their contact information and for answers to a few questions about their child. The teacher should then follow up with an email or phone call within the first month of school so the parent or caregiver knows the teacher is aware of his or her child, is paying attention, and wants to connect the bridge between home and school.

Further this partnership by continuing communication throughout the year. Newsletters, emails, websites, and phone calls are all excellent methods of communication. If there are families whose primary language is not English, try to send home newsletters in the primary language. If that is not possible, offer other ways to communicate that may be easier. Hold conferences at various times of the day to accommodate working parents. Some teachers even make home visits, when necessary. Getting the parents on your side and putting them in a position of support is a critical aspect of teaching. Most parents want to help their children

Research has consistently shown that the more involved families are, the more motivated children are to succeed and the more they do succeed. But creating these partnerships can be challenging. Parents may want to be involved but may find it difficult. Perhaps they work full time, speak another language, or have multiple children who need lots of attention.

succeed, but it is up to the teacher to find the most efficient way to make this happen.

SKILL 10.5.4 — Partnerships with the community

The community is the backbone of the morale of the children. What priorities does the community have? Is it evident that education is one of them? A strong community will show its support through fundraisers, attendance at school functions, advertisements for school fundraisers, and general appreciation and support for the teachers and administrators. Teachers can make this partnership more effective by participating in community/school events, staying active in the community themselves, and supporting their students when they can. It may not always be possible, but if a student invites a teacher to his football or soccer game, the teacher may consider attending. When everyone comes together to support the children, the children will have more motivation—and therefore, more success.

SKILL 10.6 — Knows basic strategies for developing collaborative relationships with colleagues, administrators, other school personnel, parents/caregivers, and the community to support the educational process

The most important aspect of creating a collaborative relationship is open and nonjudgmental communication. Communication must occur in various ways so that all stakeholders have an opportunity to weigh in, if they would like to. These may include emails, phone calls, newsletters, podcasts, websites, or blog posts. Occasional surveys or face-to-face seminars also may be helpful in gaining information from stakeholders.

The key is not only to be available but also to be open to communication and to other points of views. There will be times when stakeholders completely disagree, but the person in the higher position should always treat the others with respect and kindness. This type of interaction will help the others feel heard and respected, even if there are disagreements.

There is a fine line to walk between certain stakeholders, especially between parent and teacher and between administrator and teacher. Some information is confidential and cannot be shared. However, the person who is questioning a decision may not understand that and may push the other stakeholder to answer questions that he cannot. This can create tension and miscommunication. The best strategy in this case is for the administrator or teacher to be honest and explain the situation and current challenges as well as possible without sharing confidential information.

> ### SKILL 10.6.1 Knows the elements of successful collaboration, such as developing an action plan, identifying the stakeholders, identifying the purpose of the collaboration, supporting effective communication, seeking support

Throughout a teaching career, an educator may find issues he wishes to explore further and may conduct action research to solve a problem he sees in his classroom or even in his school. The teacher also may choose to adjust curriculum or assessments or add to the student experience, and all of these efforts will require successful collaboration. Before the teacher begins the project, he must identify the problem the project is intended to address. Often, teachers run toward a solution without first defining the problem. Talk to all stakeholders to try to consider as many perspectives as possible. Discuss the situation, ask questions, and discuss multiple solution options with stakeholders. Next, be sure to keep the purpose of the research in mind when creating the solution and determining which path to follow for solution implementation.

> ### SKILL 10.7 Understands the implications of major legislation and court decisions relating to students and teachers, such as equal access, privacy and confidentiality, First Amendment issues, intellectual freedom, mandated reporting of child neglect/abuse, due process, liability, licensing, tenure, copyright

Equal Access/Privacy/Confidentiality: There are three major pieces of legislation with which every educator should be familiar.

Family Educational Rights and Privacy Act (FERPA): This law is focused on confidentiality. Student records are kept in locked cabinets and are kept confidential from the general public. Parents may request access to them, but they are to be kept in the main office. Student records include anything having to do with the child's behavior, academic progress, or test scores. If a student is transferring to a new school, the previous school has the right to release the records to the new school.

Individuals with Disabilities Education Act (IDEA): All children have the right to receive a Free Appropriate Public Education (FAPE). Any student who receives services with disabilities may not be discriminated against. Additionally, any student who is suspected of having a learning, behavioral, or developmental disability must be evaluated, free of charge, by the district.

Title IX of Educational Amendment of 1972: Title IX is a piece of legislation focused on gender. A person cannot be discriminated against based on his or her gender. Often, Title IX is discussed in sports. Equal athletic opportunities must be given to males and females.

First Amendment issues/intellectual freedom: Three historic Supreme Court cases have helped define First Amendment rights in schools. Schools can be a bit more complicated, so three separate rulings have given schools guidelines for what is allowed and what is not. The three cases are the following:

Tinker v. Des Moines Independent School District **(1963):** In this case, three students wore black armbands to protest the Vietnam War. The school asked the students to remove the armbands but continued to allow students to wear other symbols. Although the case was lost at the federal level, the Supreme Court overturned the decision, saying that the armbands did not disrupt learning in any way. Therefore, schools may not forbid a freedom of expression because they disagree or do not like it; to be forbidden, the expression must disrupt the school environment or invade others' rights (http://www.firstamendmentschools.org/freedoms/faq.aspx?id=12991).

Bethel School District 403 v. Fraser **(1986):** A student gave a speech in school that was filled with lewd language. The Supreme Court ruled that students can make political speeches but cannot use lewd or vulgar language. Political messages are protected by the First Amendment, but vulgar and/or offensive speech is prohibited in schools (ibid).

Hazelwood School District v. Kuhlmeier **(1988):** Two stories, one on pregnancy and one on divorce, were printed in a school newspaper. The administration removed the stories from the paper. Eventually, the case reached the Supreme Court, where the judges decided that schools do have the right to control student content/speech if they have real concerns about the subject matter. The removal of specific subject matter must be due to legitimate concern; and if it is not, the students have the right to discuss that particular subject matter (ibid). This particular ruling has a large gray area, and it can be interpreted many ways.

> *What are the free expression rights of students in public schools under the First Amendment?* http://www.firstamendmentschools.org/freedoms/faq.aspx?id=12991 Retrieved Dec. 16, 2014.

Mandated Reporting of Child Neglect/Abuse: Teachers are mandated to report child neglect or abuse. That means that if a teacher suspects something (bruises are visible; a child complains repeatedly of not being fed, of being hurt, or of being touched inappropriately), the teacher must report it. The Keeping Children and Families Safe Act of 2003 was the reauthorization of the Child Abuse Prevention and Treatment Act, which defines child abuse and neglect. States have various rules about whom the teachers must tell, how the report must be filed, and what must be included in the report. State reporting laws can be found at http://www.childwelfare.gov/systemwide/laws_policies/state/.

Teachers do not always have to use their names when reporting, although it is best to do so when possible to make it easier for Child Protective Services (CPS) to follow up. Teachers also may share their thoughts with school administrators so they can help the teachers through this sensitive process.

It is important to note that accusing a caregiver of child abuse and/or neglect is a very serious charge. Teachers should not report a caregiver unless they are sure of the problem and have evidence to prove the claim.

Reporting child abuse and neglect.
https://www.childwelfare.gov/pubs/usermanuals/educator/educatord.cfm Retrieved Dec. 16, 2014.

Due Process: Due process has a special place in the special education world, specifically in the IEP process. Sometimes, parents or caregivers will not agree with what the teachers or therapists are saying about placement, eligibility, or services, or they may feel that their child is being treated unfairly. In this case, parents have some options. They can go through mediation, in which they and a representative meet with a neutral party to resolve the issue. If mediation doesn't work or the parents do not choose this route, they have the option of a due process hearing. In this hearing, each party provides a written commentary with evidence to make its case. Witnesses will testify, and a hearing officer will make the decision. These cases can be appealed.

Due process also applies to teachers. If a tenured teacher is dismissed, the district must go through a process to document the fairness of the dismissal. For example, a teacher must be given an oral and written warning, as well as evidence describing the decision, prior to termination.

Teachers' Rights: Tenure and Dismissal
http://education.findlaw.com/teachers-rights/teachers-rights-tenure-and-dismissal.html Retrieved Dec. 16, 2014.

Understanding IEP Due Process
http://www.understandingspecialeducation.com/IEP-due-process.html Retrieved Dec. 16, 2014.

Liability/Copyright: Both teachers and students are responsible for liability and copyright issues. Students need to be aware that anything they quote or paraphrase is not their own work and therefore must be cited in a paper or presentation. This is especially true when using the Internet. Often a student may find something online and quickly paraphrase it; however, the student still must cite the website as a source (unless the information is common knowledge, in which case citations are not necessary). Students also should be taught how to find the correct citation for the source. Sometimes, especially on the Internet, that may mean contacting the source.

In this technological age, teachers face more copyright issues than ever before. With copious amounts of information at their fingertips, it's still important for students to cite sources, never copy material that explicitly states that it is forbidden, and not to post anything online unless it is original work.

It is important to keep in mind that if a teacher violates a copyright law, the teacher's district is responsible. This can mean lawsuits or uncomfortable situations for stakeholders.

District liability and teaching responsibility
http://www.educationworld.com/a_curr/curr280e.shtml
Retrieved Dec. 16, 2014.

Licensing: Before a teacher is licensed to teach in a state, the teacher must have received a certificate from the state department of education that states that she has passed all of the requirements. The requirements may include a test, (such as this one!), coursework, or even student teaching or observation. Often, educators who move from state to state will have to apply for licensing in the new state. This could be as simple as filling out paperwork or as difficult as completing additional coursework and taking a new exam. When the teacher has become licensed, especially for the first time, he will receive a temporary license that is only good for a few years. During that time, most often he will be asked to complete more coursework, a mentor program, or a portfolio to show documentation of his growth as a teacher. After these are completed, he may be awarded a more permanent license, which will still need to be renewed every few years with extra paperwork.

Every state has different requirements for teacher licensing, so it's important to check with the state department of education before applying for jobs, because schools often cannot hire teachers until they have received at least a temporary educator's license.

Tenure: In most states, there is a law that protects tenured teachers from being dismissed without cause. Once a teacher is considered tenured, she is automatically renewed each year. If that teacher is dismissed, it must be due to a legitimate cause, not just at the district's discretion, and the district must go through due process before any final decisions are made.

Teachers' Rights: Tenure and Dismissal
http://education.findlaw.com/teachers-rights/teachers-rights-tenure-and-dismissal.html
Retrieved Dec. 16, 2014.

SAMPLE TEST

(Average) (Skill 1.1)

1. **It is important for teachers to understand a child's background schema, because:**

   A. Background schema measures how much knowledge a child has

   B. Background schema provides the foundation of a child's knowledge, created through experiences

   C. Background schema explains a child's cultural background

   D. Piaget says that background schema is an excellent measure of cognitive development

(Easy) (Skill 1.1)

2. **Lev Vygotsky was an educational theorist in which of the following philosophies?**

   A. Behaviorism

   B. Constructivism

   C. Socialism

   D. Cognitivism

(Average) (Skill 1.1)

3. **If a child is metacognitive, it means that she:**

   A. Knows how she learns

   B. Knows what her cognitive processes look like

   C. Knows how she uses her cognitive processes to gain knowledge

   D. All of the above

(Easy) (Skill 1.2)

4. **The acronyms "ZPD" and "MKO" are part of which educational theorist's ideas?**

   A. Piaget

   B. Bruner

   C. Vygotsky

   D. Bloom

(Rigorous) (Skill 1.2)

5. **The second stage of Piaget's four stages is called:**

   A. The preoperational stage

   B. The sensorimotor stage

   C. The formal operational stage

   D. The concrete operational stage

(Rigorous) (Skill 1.2)

6. **If a two-year-old child does not eat a cookie before dinner because he is afraid he will be punished if he breaks the "no cookie before dinner" rule, he is in which stage of Kohlberg's moral development?**

   A. Conventional morality

   B. Preconventional morality

   C. Postconventional morality

   D. None of the above

(Average) (Skill 1.2)

7. **The highest level of Bloom's revised taxonomy is:**

   A. Applying

   B. Analyzing

   C. Creating

   D. Evaluating

(Rigorous) (Skill 1.2)

8. Who is responsible for the self-efficacy theory?

   A. Vygotsky

   B. Piaget

   C. Dewey

   D. Bandura

(Rigorous) (Skill 1.3)

9. These two concepts are similar in definition; both discuss how a person connects a familiar concept to a new concept.

   A. Background schema and transfer

   B. Transfer and self-efficacy

   C. Background schema and self-efficacy

   D. Zone of proximal development and self-regulation

(Average) (Skill 1.3)

10. Why do young children struggle with self-regulation?

    A. Young children don't have patience

    B. Young children have little control over their impulses and don't yet fully understand the consequences of their actions

    C. Young children are not good listeners

    D. Young children don't appreciate authority

(Easy) (Skill 1.4)

11. The major cognitive theorist is:

    A. Vygotsky

    B. Bloom

    C. Bruner

    D. Piaget

(Average) (Skill 1.4)

12. According to Piaget, a three- to five-year-old will be focusing on learning:

    A. Language skills

    B. Gross and fine motor skills

    C. Handwriting

    D. Working with screens

(Easy) (Skill 1.4)

13. An infant shows his displeasure by:

    A. Crying

    B. Talking

    C. Sleeping

    D. Smiling

(Rigorous) (Skill 1.5)

14. What developmental theory explains why two kindergartners will fight over a specific toy, but by first grade, this argument will have lessened?

    A. Piaget's stages of cognitive development

    B. Bloom's stages of understanding

    C. Kohlberg's stages of moral development

    D. None of the above

(Easy) (Skill 2.2.2)

15. The following are categories for exceptional students:

    A. Autism

    B. Deaf/blind

    C. Intellectual disability

    D. All of the above

(Average) (Skill 2.3)

16. The three major laws that apply to special needs students are:

    A. No Child Left Behind, ADA, and IDEA

    B. IDEA, ADA, and Section 504

    C. IDEA, Section 504, and No Child Left Behind

    D. None of the above

(Easy) (Skill 2.3)

17. **An IEP meeting is called for students:**

    A. Who have documented disabilities

    B. Who have failed a test

    C. Whose parents want to meet with a teacher

    D. Who don't speak English

(Rigorous) (Skill 2.4)

18. **Gifted students include those who:**

    A. Have a high level of ability and achievement

    B. Have a low level of ability and achievement

    C. Have a documented learning disability

    D. Both A and C

(Easy) (Skill 2.4)

19. **Characteristics of gifted students may include:**

    A. Perfectionism

    B. Abstract thinking

    C. Heightened sensitivity to their own expectations

    D. All of the above

(Average) (Skill 2.5)

20. **The theorist responsible for the term "culturally responsive classroom" is:**

    A. Lev Vygotsky

    B. Gloria Ladson-Billings

    C. Benjamin Bloom

    D. John Dewey

(Easy) (Skill 2.6.1)

21. **Exceptionalities means:**

    A. Differences

    B. All students with disabilities

    C. All gifted students

    D. None of the above

(Average) (Skill 2.6.2)

22. **Why would a student take a test in a small group?**

    A. The student is not interested in the material and needs motivation

    B. The student loses focus, and a small group can help minimize distraction

    C. A small group can allow the teacher to give more individualized attention to each student

    D. Both A and C

(Average) (Skill 3.1)

23. **The most important level of Maslow's hierarchy is:**

    A. Belongingness

    B. Psychological

    C. Self-actualization

    D. Physiological

(Average) (Skill 3.1)

24. **Erik Erikson is known for his theory of:**

    A. Operant versus classical conditioning

    B. Eight stages of psychosocial development

    C. The zone of proximal development

    D. Multiple intelligences

(Rigorous) (Skill 3.1)

25. **The "father of behaviorism" is:**

    A. Skinner

    B. Dewey

    C. Watson

    D. Maslow

(Rigorous) (Skill 3.1)

26. **"A response that is given a satisfactory outcome will be repeated, while a response that incurs a negative outcome will be less likely to happen again in the future." This is the definition of which theory?**

    A. Operant conditioning

    B. Classical conditioning

    C. Law of effect

    D. Behaviorism

(Average) (Skill 3.2.1)

27. **The following terms relate to which theory? Self-determination, attribution, self-efficacy, classical and operant conditioning**

    A. Behaviorism

    B. Motivation

    C. Zone of proximal development

    D. None of the above

(Easy) (Skill 3.2.1)

28. **If a child performs in school because she wants a sticker promised by the teacher, she is motivated:**

    A. Intrinsically

    B. Extrinsically

    C. Neither intrinsically nor extrinsically

    D. Both intrinsically and extrinsically

(Rigorous) (Skill 3.2.1)

29. **Henry loves ocean life. He has categorized all sea life as fish. Henry's teacher tells him that a whale is not a fish, but actually is a mammal. Henry does not understand how this could be true. This is an example of:**

    A. Classical conditioning

    B. Law of effect

    C. Cognitive dissonance

    D. Attribution

(Average) (Skill 3.2.1)

30. **Which type of conditioning is based on involuntary behaviors?**

    A. Classical conditioning

    B. Operant conditioning

    C. Both

    D. Neither

(Average) (Skill 3.2.1)

31. Lucy raises her hand to answer a question, and the teacher responds by saying, "Great job raising your hand!" This response is an example of:

    A. Operant conditioning

    B. Classical conditioning

    C. Both

    D. Neither

(Easy) (Skill 3.3.2)

32. Mr. Diaz has a class full of students who do not want to learn. They are unruly and do not follow class rules. To help them become motivated, Mr. Diaz decides to use a token economy in his class. This is an example of:

    A. Intrinsic motivation

    B. Extrinsic motivation

    C. Both

    D. Neither

(Easy) (Skill 3.3)

33. Why would a teacher stand outside her classroom door and welcome her students each day?

    A. It sets the tone for a caring and positive environment

    B. She can make sure students have brought supplies to class

    C. She can take attendance

    D. All of the above

(Average) (Skill 3.3)

34. When should a teacher begin safety drills?

    A. In the first month of school

    B. In the first week of school

    C. On the first day of school

    D. By the end of the first quarter

(Average) (Skill 3.3)

35. Learning Center directions should be:

    A. Clear

    B. Concise

    C. Colorful

    D. All of the above

(Easy) (Skill 3.3.2)

36. Why must a teacher maintain accurate records?

    A. For academic purposes

    B. For behavior purposes

    C. For parent communication

    D. All of the above

(Average) (Skill 3.4.1)

37. The following is an example of an authentic assignment.

    A. Homework

    B. Silent reading

    C. Question and answer

    D. A mock trial

(Average) (Skill 3.4.2)

38. **A good example of positive feedback would be:**

    A. "Great job!"

    B. "I love how you colored in the lines today."

    C. "You made a good effort."

    D. "You didn't do well on this assignment."

(Rigorous) (Skill 3.4.3)

39. **A good example of a written objective for students is:**

    A. Today we will learn about counting money.

    B. Today we are going to add money because you need it when you go shopping.

    C. Today we are learning the difference between a dime and a quarter. This is important when we are trying to tell the difference between coins.

    D. Today we are learning how a dime and a quarter are different. We are doing this so we don't get confused.

(Rigorous) (Skill 4.1.1)

40. **Why do we have national standards?**

    A. To keep teachers on the same instructional track

    B. To track student progress

    C. To give each child the opportunity for an equal education

    D. Because No Child Left Behind mandates it

(Average) (Skill 4.1.2)

41. **Where can a teacher find national and state standards for her grade level?**

    A. On the department of education website

    B. In the school office

    C. On the school website

    D. In her classroom

(Rigorous) (Skill 4.2.1)

42. **The type of memory that is processed the fastest is:**

    A. Sensory memory

    B. Long-term memory

    C. Working memory

    D. None of the above

(Average) (Skill 4.2.1)

43. **When someone visualizes information in the mind for easier recall, that is called:**

    A. Background schema

    B. Mapping

    C. Sensory memory

    D. Long-term memory

(Rigorous) (Skill 4.2.2)

44. **Juan sees that his friend Lucy is listening carefully to the teacher. Normally, when the teacher is talking, Juan likes to make his neighbor, Carlos, laugh. Often, this gets him in trouble. But today, he sees that Lucy is listening intently and taking notes. When she raises her hand, the**

teacher praises her. Juan decides to raise his hand, and he gets called on and praised. Then, he decides to stop talking with Carlos and instead tries to listen to the lesson. This type of behavior is called:

A. Modeling

B. Vicarious learning

C. Reciprocal determinism

D. Both B and C

(Rigorous) (Skill 4.3.1)

45. Mrs. Jones is about to begin a unit on the Middle Ages. She will cover the basics of the political, economic, and social struggles of the Middle Ages. Students also will learn about the music, clothing, and class systems. This short description covers:

A. The scope of the unit

B. The sequence of the unit

C. Both the scope and sequence

D. Neither the scope or sequence

(Rigorous) (Skill 4.5.1)

46. An excellent example of how cognition moves from elementary to more advanced is:

A. Vygotsky's ZPD

B. Bloom's taxonomy

C. Gardner's multiple intelligences

D. Dewey's social theory

(Rigorous) (Skill 4.5.1)

47. A child who is developing jumping, running, and handwriting is working on her:

A. Affective domain

B. Psychomotor domain

C. Interpersonal domain

D. None of the above

(Average) (Skill 4.5.3)

48. Observable behavior may include:

A. How much Timothy likes math

B. How often Javier raised his hand during math

C. How many times Javier answered correctly

D. Both B and C

(Easy) (Skill 4.5.4)

49. Which word would NOT be useful in writing a measurable objective?

A. Describe

B. Evaluate

C. Create

D. Learn

(Easy) (Skill 4.6.1)

50. If a child is struggling in reading and has a low performance on many assessments, he needs:

A. Enrichment

B. Remediation

C. No interventions

D. Peer tutoring

(Average) (Skill 4.7.3)

51. **A group of lessons centered on the geography of the Far East would be categorized as:**

    A. A thematic unit

    B. An interdisciplinary unit

    C. Using models

    D. Formative assessments

(Average) (Skill 4.7.5)

52. **What is the purpose of interdisciplinary instruction?**

    A. It gives students an in-depth understanding of a topic

    B. It provides real-life experience

    C. It gives students a well-rounded, view of a topic from multiple perspectives

    D. All of the above

(Average) (Skill 4.7.6)

53. **Which is a challenge that interdisciplinary teachers may face?**

    A. Lack of teacher interest

    B. Lack of student interest

    C. Teacher protectiveness

    D. Difficulty of teamwork

(Average) (Skill 4.7.7)

54. **A good use of a para educator's time is:**

    A. Making copies

    B. Managing student behavior

    C. Working with the most difficult students

    D. Managing a center

(Rigorous) (Skill 5.1)

55. **Louise always gets straight As. She does well on every assessment and is engaged in class. Her teacher wants to find out why this is happening. She looks at Louise's home life and her peer relationships and talks with her to find the answer. This type of analysis is called:**

    A. Inductive reasoning

    B. Deductive reasoning

    C. Questioning

    D. Critical thinking

(Average) (Skill 5.1)

56. **The first thing a student should see when she walks into the classroom is:**

    A. The homework for that day

    B. The behavior incentive chart

    C. The goals and objectives for that day

    D. Seatwork

(Easy) (Skill 5.1)

57. **Basic recall is:**

    A. A high level of comprehension

    B. The ability to synthesize

    C. An elementary understanding of concepts

    D. The ability to evaluate

(Easy) (Skill 5.2.1)

58. **If a teacher stands in front of the class and shows a PowerPoint presentation on a topic, he is using which type of instruction?**

    A. Direct instruction

    B. Indirect instruction

    C. Independent instruction

    D. Experiential instruction

(Average) (Skill 5.2.1)

59. **Homework is which type of instruction?**

   A. Direct instruction

   B. Indirect instruction

   C. Independent instruction

   D. Experiential instruction

(Average) (Skill 5.3.1)

60. **How long should an average lecture be for elementary students?**

   A. 10–15 minutes

   B. 15–20 minutes

   C. 30 minutes

   D. 45 minutes

(Average) (Skill 5.3.2)

61. **Inquiry learning is most useful in which subject area?**

   A. English

   B. Science

   C. Math

   D. Social Studies

(Rigorous) (Skill 5.3.2)

62. **The following is an example of which literacy strategy?**

   "Joe loves books. In fact, Joe has many _____ at his house. Many of the books are about horses and farms. _____ are places where animals live."

   A. Reading for meaning

   B. Running records

   C. Cloze procedures

   D. None of the above

(Average) (Skill 5.3.4)

63. **All of the following are examples of experiential learning EXCEPT:**

   A. Field trips

   B. Direct instruction

   C. Role play

   D. Experiments

(Easy) (Skill 5.3.5)

64. **Brainstorming should be done at what point in the writing process?**

   A. At the beginning

   B. At the end

   C. In the middle of drafting

   D. Whenever the child needs it

(Rigorous) (Skill 5.4.1)

65. **When a student associates multiplication with addition, she is showing which type of learning?**

   A. Collaborative learning

   B. Problem solving

   C. Transfer learning

   D. Critical thinking

(Easy) (Skill 5.4.2)

66. **When a student is comparing two stories, she should look for:**

   A. Similarities

   B. Differences

   C. Both

   D. Neither

(Average) (Skill 5.4.2)

67. When a small child sorts toys by color, she is showing which type of cognitive learning?

   A. Predicting

   B. Categorizing

   C. Analyzing

   D. Contrasting

(Rigorous) (Skill 5.4.2)

68. When a teacher asks her students to perform a picture walk, she is asking them to use which skill?

   A. Summarizing

   B. Decision making

   C. Sequencing

   D. Inferring

(Average) (Skill 5.5.1)

69. A young child who is told not to eat a cookie but then eats it as soon as the adult walks away does not have very strong skills in which area?

   A. Scaffolding

   B. Modeling

   C. Self-regulation

   D. None of the above

(Average) (Skill 5.5.1)

70. Mr. Cameron sets up three centers in his room, each of which practices rhyming. The first center asks students to play a matching game. The second asks students to write a poem, and the third is a teacher-run center where students jump on words that rhyme. Mr. Cameron is practicing which type of instruction?

   A. Differentiated instruction

   B. Guided practice

   C. Scaffolding

   D. Coaching

Case History I (Questions CR 1–2)

Scenario: Mrs. Dodd, a young, white female, is a third-year fifth-grade teacher. She was hired this year at a low-income suburban school, where most of the students are of a different ethnicity and cultural and socioeconomic background than she is. She has one class that has 27 students in it, and 12 of these students perform below grade level. She has tried to motivate her students with the techniques she used in the past, but her other school had a higher socioeconomic population, and students were motivated by grades or parent intervention. Her students don't respond to the threat of low grades, and many of the parents are not involved. Additionally, she is having trouble controlling student behavior and is struggling to give her students the academic attention they need.

Document 1

Ethnography of Mrs. Dodd's third-period class:

27 students
12 black students
8 white students
5 Hispanic students
2 classified as other

4 students are English Language Learners

12 students did not pass the state exam last year

20 students are on free/reduced lunch

Document 2

Mrs. Dodd's classroom management plan:

On the wall, in student sight, there is a poster with the following rules:

1. Respect one another and yourself
2. Raise your hand before speaking
3. Come to class prepared

Mrs. Dodd begins the class by placing the number 10 on the board. When students make a good choice, she adds to that number. When they make a poor choice, she takes away from that number. At the end of the period, the number remaining is how many minutes of free time students receive. Often, the class receives between two and four minutes.

Document 3

Notes on particular students from Mrs. Dodd's journal:

1. Alex: Alex is a class leader. He enters the class loudly and high-fives his friends. His seat is at the front, and he saunters to the front, trying to get everyone's attention in the process. The class gets louder as he enters. Academically, Alex is far behind, but he acts silly whenever he is presented with new information. He speaks out of turn and interrupts me as I teach, and I have to ask him to sit outside the classroom a few days a week so I can continue my lesson without interruption.

2. Madison: Madison sits by herself and doesn't participate. She is a smart girl but sometimes says disrespectful things under her breath. Often, I send her outside to sit for a few minutes. She turns in high-quality work, but she seems bored and distracted.

3. Logan: Logan is a quiet ringleader. He plays football, and students know him as an athlete, but he is far behind academically. Once a week, his mentor comes to class with him and sits by him. The rest of the class doesn't know why the mentor is there, but it distracts them. Logan makes other students laugh and generally is disrespectful.

Document 4

Notes from Mr. Brown, the principal, after meeting with Mrs. Dodd:

Mrs. Dodd is a professional teacher who appears to be struggling. She has great intentions, and she wants her students to succeed. However, the strategies she used at her previous school do not work here. We have a different type of population than she is used to. She believes her students don't respect her. She mentioned that they rarely come to class prepared, and they speak out of turn, interrupt her, and misbehave. Additionally, she has a few students in the class who are academically needy, and a few others who are bored with the curriculum. Currently, she has one paraprofessional in there with her, but she has requested more help. I believe that if she has a chance to meet with her mentor teacher and come up with a plan, Mrs. Dodd can be a more effective teacher to this struggling class.

CR 1: Mrs. Dodd's classroom ethnography may give some insight as to why Mrs. Dodd is struggling.

Examine the ethnography of Mrs. Dodd's class. Explain TWO challenges she may face.

Describe and explain two strategies she could use to create a more culturally responsive classroom.

CR 2: Mrs. Dodd is struggling with classroom management. She is having trouble controlling her students, and it's hurting her students academically.

Describe TWO management problems Mrs. Dodd is having her in classroom, and suggest TWO solutions to these problems.

For each of these solutions, describe why these management solutions will be the most appropriate for this class and the particular behavioral issues that Mrs. Dodd is facing. Base your answers on foundations of classroom management and on out-of-the-box strategies Mrs. Dodd can use.

ANSWER KEY						
1. B	11. D	21. A	31. A	41. A	51. A	61. B
2. B	12. B	22. B	32. B	42. A	52. D	62. C
3. D	13. A	23. D	33. A	43. B	53. C	63. B
4. C	14. C	24. B	34. B	44. D	54. D	64. A
5. A	15. D	25. C	35. D	45. A	55. A	65. C
6. B	16. B	26. C	36. D	46. B	56. C	66. A
7. C	17. A	27. B	37. D	47. B	57. C	67. B
8. D	18. D	28. B	38. B	48. D	58. A	68. D
9. A	19. D	29. C	39. C	49. D	59. C	69. C
10. B	20. B	30. A	40. C	50. B	60. A	70. A

RIGOR TABLE	
Rigor level	Questions
Easy 20%	11, 13, 15, 19, 21, 28, 32, 33, 36, 50, 57, 58, 64, 66
Average 40%	1, 3, 10, 12, 16, 20, 22, 23, 24, 27, 30, 31, 34, 35, 37, 38, 41, 43, 48, 51, 52, 53, 54, 56, 60, 63, 69, 70
Rigorous 40%	2, 4, 5, 6, 7, 8, 9, 14, 17, 18, 25, 26, 29, 39, 40, 42, 44, 45, 46, 47, 49, 55, 59, 61, 62, 65, 67, 68

(Average) (Skill 1.1)

1. **It is important for teachers to understand a child's background schema, because:**

   A. Background schema measures how much knowledge a child has

   B. Background schema provides the foundation of a child's knowledge, created through experiences

   C. Background schema explains a child's cultural background

   D. Piaget says that background schema is an excellent measure of cognitive development

   Answer: B. Background schema provides the foundation of a child's knowledge, created through experiences.

   Background schema is created from social and academic experiences. Students conceptualize new knowledge, and then they file it away, retrieving it when they learn new information. By comparing already familiar information to new information, students will understand concepts more quickly and with a higher comprehension level.

(Easy) (Skill 1.1)

2. **Lev Vygotsky was an educational theorist in which of the following philosophies?**

   A. Behaviorism

   B. Constructivism

   C. Socialism

   D. Cognitivism

   Answer: B. Constructivism.

   Lev Vygotsky was a constructivist philosopher. He believed that experiences and social environments form the basis for knowledge.

(Average) (Skill 1.1)

3. **If a child is metacognitive, it means that she:**

   A. Knows how she learns

   B. Knows what her cognitive processes look like

   C. Knows how she uses her cognitive processes to gain knowledge

   D. All of the above

   Answer: D. All of the above.

   Metacognition is understanding how you learn. If a person is fully metacognitive, which can take years, she will understand how she learns, what types of lessons work the best for her, and how she gains new knowledge.

(Easy) (Skill 1.2)

4. **The acronyms "ZPD" and "MKO" are part of which educational theorist's ideas?**

   A. Piaget

   B. Bruner

   C. Vygotsky

   D. Bloom

   Answer: C. Vygotsky.

   Vygotsky discussed the zone of proximal development (ZPD) and the more knowledgeable other (MKO). The ZPD is the space between independence in a skill and needing help to finish a task, and the MKO is the person who helps a student through his ZPD toward independence.

(Rigorous) (Skill 1.2)

5. **The second stage of Piaget's four stages is called:**

    A. The preoperational stage

    B. The sensorimotor stage

    C. The formal operational stage

    D. The concrete operational stage

    Answer: A. The preoperational stage.
    Children in this stage exhibit a large jump in vocabulary and expressive and receptive language development. These children see themselves as the center, and are egocentric about their lives. They will not understand concrete logic or others' points of view.

(Rigorous) (Skill 1.2)

6. **If a two-year-old child does not eat a cookie before dinner because he is afraid he will be punished if he breaks the "no cookie before dinner" rule, he is in which stage of Kohlberg's moral development?**

    A. Conventional morality

    B. Preconventional morality

    C. Postconventional morality

    D. None of the above

    Answer: B. Preconventional morality.
    The first level of Kohlberg's moral development is called preconventional morality. There are two substages, "obedience and punishment" and "individualism and exchange." According to Kohlberg, two-year-olds are in the preconventional stage of morality—specifically, the "obedience and punishment" stage. In this stage, a child will obey a rule only because he fears the consequence, not because he understands why an action is wrong.

(Average) (Skill 1.2)

7. **The highest level of Bloom's revised taxonomy is:**

    A. Applying

    B. Analyzing

    C. Creating

    D. Evaluating

    Answer: C. Creating.
    Creating is now treated as the top level of Bloom's taxonomy. If a student fully understands the concept and can combine, explain, organize, and create, he has reached the "create" level of Bloom's taxonomy.

(Rigorous) (Skill 1.2)

8. **Who is responsible for the self-efficacy theory?**

    A. Vygotsky

    B. Piaget

    C. Dewey

    D. Bandura

    Answer: D. Bandura.
    Albert Bandura is responsible for the self-efficacy theory, which states that a person's perception of his capabilities is a form of positive thinking that involves a person believing that he can accomplish certain goals.

(Rigorous) (Skill 1.3)

9. **These two concepts are similar in definition; both discuss how a person connects a familiar concept to a new concept.**

    A. Background schema and transfer

    B. Transfer and self-efficacy

    C. Background schema and self-efficacy

    D. Zone of proximal development and self-regulation

Answer: A. Background schema and transfer.

Background schema and transfer are similar. Background schema refers to the knowledge a student brings to a new concept, and transfer refers to a student's ability to connect one concept to another similar concept.

(Average) (Skill 1.3)

10. **Why do young children struggle with self-regulation?**

   A. Young children don't have patience

   B. Young children have little control over their impulses and don't yet fully understand the consequences of their actions

   C. Young children are not good listeners

   D. Young children don't appreciate authority

Answer: B. Young children have little control over their impulses and don't yet fully understand the consequences of their actions.

Although at times it may seem that young children just are not listening, they actually have little control over their impulses and often cannot understand the consequences of their actions. As they get older, they will develop self-regulation.

(Easy) (Skill 1.4)

11. **The major cognitive theorist is:**

   A. Vygotsky

   B. Bloom

   C. Bruner

   D. Piaget

Answer: D. Piaget.

Piaget created four well-known stages of cognitive development.

(Average) (Skill 1.4)

12. **According to Piaget, a three- to five-year-old will be focusing on learning:**

   A. Language skills

   B. Gross and fine motor skills

   C. Handwriting

   D. Working with screens

Answer: B. Gross and fine motor skills.

Between the ages of three and five, a child is working on her fine and gross motor skills. These skills are developing rapidly at this point in development.

(Easy) (Skill 1.4)

13. **An infant shows his displeasure by:**

   A. Crying

   B. Talking

   C. Sleeping

   D. Smiling

Answer: A. Crying.

When an infant cries, it is because he is feeling unsafe, scared, hungry, or cold. He doesn't have any other way to express his frustration, so he cries.

(Rigorous) (Skill 1.5)

14. **What developmental theory explains why two kindergartners will fight over a specific toy, but by first grade, this argument will have lessened?**

   A. Piaget's stages of cognitive development

   B. Bloom's stages of understanding

   C. Kohlberg's stages of moral development

   D. None of the above

Answer: C. Kohlberg's stages of moral development.

Kohlberg's theory of moral development explains this change. A younger child is still learning how to cooperate with others. By age six or seven, he is on to a new stage of moral development, so he is struggling with other issues and most likely has resolved the sharing frustration.

(Easy) (Skill 2.2.2)

15. **The following are categories for exceptional students:**

    A. Autism

    B. Deaf/blind

    C. Intellectual disability

    D. All of the above

Answer: D. All of the above.

All of the above are for students with exceptional needs. Others include hearing impairments, orthopedic impairments, developmental delays, and learning disabilities.

(Average) (Skill 2.3)

16. **The three major laws that apply to special needs students are:**

    A. No Child Left Behind, ADA, and IDEA

    B. IDEA, ADA, and Section 504

    C. IDEA, Section 504, and No Child Left Behind

    D. None of the above

Answer: B. IDEA, ADA, and Section 504.

These three laws are the major legislation focused on special education. IDEA, the Individuals with Disabilities Education Act, protects children from ages 3 through 21 and gives financial aid to ensure education services are available for children with documented disabilities. ADA, the Americans with Disabilities Act, protects all citizens against discrimination based on a disability. Section 504 states that no one with a documented disability can be denied acceptance into programs that receive federal financial assistance because of that disability.

(Easy) (Skill 2.3)

17. **An IEP meeting is called for students:**

    A. Who have documented disabilities

    B. Who have failed a test

    C. Whose parents want to meet with a teacher

    D. Who don't speak English

Answer: A. Who have documented disabilities.

An IEP meeting is called when a student has a documented disability or is moving through the testing process. IEP stands for "individualized education plan." IEPs are created for students who have been tested and documented as needing specific services.

(Rigorous) (Skill 2.4)

18. **Gifted students include those who:**

    A. Have a high level of ability and achievement

    B. Have a low level of ability and achievement

    C. Have a documented learning disability

    D. Both A and C

Answer: D. Both A and C.

It is possible for a student to be identified as gifted and to have a documented learning disability. Most students identified as gifted have a high level of ability and achievement. However, many students who have a high level of ability and achievement may struggle in another aspect of school.

(Easy) (Skill 2.4)

19. **Characteristics of gifted students may include:**

    A. Perfectionism

    B. Abstract thinking

    C. Heightened sensitivity to their own expectations

    D. All of the above

    Answer: D. All of the above.
    According to the National Society for the Gifted and Talented, all of the above are characteristics of a gifted child.

(Average) (Skill 2.5)

20. **The theorist responsible for the term "culturally responsive classroom" is:**

    A. Lev Vygotsky

    B. Gloria Ladson-Billings

    C. Benjamin Bloom

    D. John Dewey

    Answer: B. Gloria Ladson-Billings.
    Gloria Ladson-Billings advocated for a culturally responsive classroom in which students are looked at holistically, taking into account their rich and distinctive culture and home literacies. This is particularly important for English Language Learners.

(Easy) (Skill 2.6.1)

21. **Exceptionalities means:**

    A. Differences

    B. All students with disabilities

    C. All gifted students

    D. None of the above

Answer: A. Differences.
Simply, exceptionalities means differences.

(Average) (Skill 2.6.2)

22. **Why would a student take a test in a small group?**

    A. The student is not interested in the material and needs motivation

    B. The student loses focus, and a small group can help minimize distraction

    C. A small group can allow the teacher to give more individualized attention to each student

    D. Both A and C

    Answer: B. The student loses focus, and a small group can help minimize distraction.
    Often, a student is placed in a small group to minimize distraction. It is important to note that in standardized state tests, the teacher is not allowed to give the students any help, so it is important for teachers to know the rules of each assessment prior to administering it.

(Average) (Skill 3.1)

23. **The most important level of Maslow's hierarchy is:**

    A. Belongingness

    B. Psychological

    C. Self-actualization

    D. Physiological

    Answer: D. Physiological.
    Physiological needs, which include food, shelter, water, and sleep, are the most basic and most important. When these needs are not met, a child will not be able to learn anything academic, because she will be focused on survival.

(Average) (Skill 3.1)

24. **Erik Erikson is known for his theory of:**

    A. Operant versus classical conditioning

    B. Eight stages of psychosocial development

    C. The zone of proximal development

    D. Multiple intelligences

    Answer: B. Eight stages of psychosocial development.
    Erik Erikson developed the eight psychosocial stages through which a person will progress in his lifetime. When he succeeds in one stage, he will move to the next.

(Rigorous) (Skill 3.1)

25. **The "father of behaviorism" is:**

    A. Skinner

    B. Dewey

    C. Watson

    D. Maslow

    Answer: C. Watson.
    John Watson coined the term behaviorism, which means that nurture is responsible for creating a person's strengths and weaknesses.

(Rigorous) (Skill 3.1)

26. **"A response that is given a satisfactory outcome will be repeated, while a response that incurs a negative outcome will be less likely to happen again in the future." This is the definition of which theory?**

    A. Operant conditioning

    B. Classical conditioning

    C. Law of effect

    D. Behaviorism

Answer: C. Law of effect.
Edward Thorndike developed this theory, which is known as the law of effect.

(Average) (Skill 3.2.1)

27. **The following terms relate to which theory? Self-determination, attribution, self-efficacy, classical and operant conditioning**

    A. Behaviorism

    B. Motivation

    C. Zone of proximal development

    D. None of the above

    Answer: B. Motivation.
    All these ideas are related to motivation theory.

(Easy) (Skill 3.2.1)

28. **If a child performs in school because she wants a sticker promised by the teacher, she is motivated:**

    A. Intrinsically

    B. Extrinsically

    C. Neither intrinsically nor extrinsically

    D. Both intrinsically and extrinsically

    Answer: B. Extrinsically.
    A child who is motivated by extrinsic factors is motivated by rewards or prizes, such as stickers, candy, or grades.

(Rigorous) (Skill 3.2.1)

29. Henry loves ocean life. He has categorized all sea life as fish. Henry's teacher tells him that a whale is not a fish, but actually is a mammal. Henry does not understand how this could be true. This is an example of:

    A. Classical conditioning

    B. Law of effect

    C. Cognitive dissonance

    D. Attribution

    Answer: C. Cognitive dissonance.
    Cognitive dissonance is when a child has a disconnect between what he knows and what he is trying to learn. In this example, Henry already has categorized whales as fish, but this is not true.

(Average) (Skill 3.2.1)

30. **Which type of conditioning is based on involuntary behaviors?**

    A. Classical conditioning

    B. Operant conditioning

    C. Both

    D. Neither

    Answer: A. Classical conditioning.
    Classical conditioning focuses on placing a signal before an involuntary behavior. Operant conditioning deals with reinforcing or punishing specific behaviors to solicit a particular response.

(Average) (Skill 3.2.1)

31. Lucy raises her hand to answer a question, and the teacher responds by saying, "Great job raising your hand!" This response is an example of:

    A. Operant conditioning

    B. Classical conditioning

    C. Both

    D. Neither

    Answer: A. Operant conditioning.
    By complimenting Lucy and reinforcing her behavior to the entire class, the teacher is using operant conditioning. Lucy will continue to use this behavior because she knows the teacher likes it. Also, other students may raise their hands in hopes of receiving compliments.

(Easy) (Skill 3.3.2)

32. Mr. Diaz has a class full of students who do not want to learn. They are unruly and do not follow class rules. To help them become motivated, Mr. Diaz decides to use a token economy in his class. This is an example of:

    A. Intrinsic motivation

    B. Extrinsic motivation

    C. Both

    D. Neither

    Answer: B. Extrinsic motivation.
    A token economy, in which students earn "money" for behaviors and then can buy items with that earned "money," is an example of an extrinsic motivator.

(Easy) (Skill 3.3)

33. **Why would a teacher stand outside her classroom door and welcome her students each day?**

    A. It sets the tone for a caring and positive environment

    B. She can make sure students have brought supplies to class

    C. She can take attendance

    D. All of the above

    Answer: A. It sets the tone for a caring and positive environment.
    When a teacher stands at the door and welcomes her students, she is setting the tone for a positive and caring environment. Her students will know that she cares and will feel more engaged from the first minute of class.

(Average) (Skill 3.3)

34. **When should a teacher begin safety drills?**

    A. In the first month of school

    B. In the first week of school

    C. On the first day of school

    D. By the end of the first quarter

    Answer: B. In the first week of school.
    Within the first week of school, the teacher should have explained safety procedures and practiced them with the class. The teacher should do this before the school does an all-school drill, which will happen within the first month and at other times throughout the school year.

(Average) (Skill 3.3)

35. **Learning Center directions should be:**

    A. Clear

    B. Concise

    C. Colorful

    D. All of the above

    Answer: D. All of the above.
    Learning Center directions should be clear, concise, and colorful to hold student interest and give children many opportunities to understand.

(Easy) (Skill 3.3.2)

36. **Why must a teacher maintain accurate records?**

    A. For academic purposes

    B. For behavior purposes

    C. For parent communication

    D. All of the above

    Answer: D. All of the above.
    These all are important reasons to keep accurate records.

(Average) (Skill 3.4.1)

37. **The following is an example of an authentic assignment.**

    A. Homework

    B. Silent reading

    C. Question and answer

    D. A mock trial

    Answer: D. A mock trial.
    A mock trial will engage students in what could be a real-life experience. In this situation, the teacher acts as facilitator, not as a direct instructor. This is the definition of an authentic assignment.

(Average) (Skill 3.4.2)

38. **A good example of positive feedback would be:**

    A. "Great job!"

    B. "I love how you colored in the lines today."

    C. "You made a good effort."

    D. "You didn't do well on this assignment."

    Answer: B. "I love how you colored in the lines today."
    Strong positive feedback will be short but very specific to the child's task. When a child hears exactly what she's done well, she will be more apt to repeat the behavior.

(Rigorous) (Skill 3.4.3)

39. **A good example of a written objective for students is:**

    A. Today we will learn about counting money.

    B. Today we are going to add money because you need it when you go shopping.

    C. Today we are learning the difference between a dime and a quarter. This is important when we are trying to tell the difference between coins.

    D. Today we are learning how a dime and a quarter are different. We are doing this so we don't get confused.

    Answer: C. Today we are learning the difference between a dime and a quarter. This is important when we are trying to tell the difference between coins.
    A written objective will state the "what" and the "why." Additionally, the "what" will be exact and simple, and the "why" will relate to a student's life and experiences.

(Rigorous) (Skill 4.1.1)

40. **Why do we have national standards?**

    A. To keep teachers on the same instructional track

    B. To track student progress

    C. To give each child the opportunity for an equal education

    D. Because No Child Left Behind mandates it

    Answer: C. To give each child the opportunity for an equal education.
    The theory behind national standards is to give all students the opportunity for an equal education, regardless of socioeconomic background, race, or gender.

(Average) (Skill 4.1.2)

41. **Where can a teacher find national and state standards for her grade level?**

    A. On the department of education website

    B. In the school office

    C. On the school website

    D. In her classroom

    Answer: A. On the department of education website.
    All standards for each state will be on the department of education website for that state. They also may be found in the school office, but always will be online for research purposes.

(Rigorous) (Skill 4.2.1)

42. The type of memory that is processed the fastest is:

   A. Sensory memory

   B. Long-term memory

   C. Working memory

   D. None of the above

Answer: A. Sensory memory.
Sensory memory is the quickest. When new information comes in, children process it quickly. There is a limited amount of space for sensory memory.

(Average) (Skill 4.2.1)

43. When someone visualizes information in the mind for easier recall, that is called:

   A. Background schema

   B. Mapping

   C. Sensory memory

   D. Long-term memory

Answer: B. Mapping.
Mapping is useful when students need to conceptualize information and store it in a more permanent memory.

(Rigorous) (Skill 4.2.2)

44. Juan sees that his friend Lucy is listening carefully to the teacher. Normally, when the teacher is talking, Juan likes to make his neighbor, Carlos, laugh. Often, this gets him in trouble. But today, he sees that Lucy is listening intently and taking notes. When she raises her hand, the teacher praises her. Juan decides to raise his hand, and he gets called on and praised. Then, he decides to stop talking with Carlos and instead tries to listen to the lesson. This type of behavior is called:

   A. Modeling

   B. Vicarious learning

   C. Reciprocal determinism

   D. Both B and C

Answer: D. Both B and C.
Vicarious learning is when a child sees a behavior (Lucy's good listening) and chooses to replicate it based on the consequences it receives (teacher praise). Reciprocal determinism is when a person changes his behavior based on reactions from others. Usually, Juan gets in trouble, but today, when he changes his behavior, he receives praise.

(Rigorous) (Skill 4.3.1)

45. Mrs. Jones is about to begin a unit on the Middle Ages. She will cover the basics of the political, economic, and social struggles of the Middle Ages. Students also will learn about the music, clothing, and class systems. This short description covers:

   A. The scope of the unit

   B. The sequence of the unit

   C. Both the scope and sequence

   D. Neither the scope or sequence

Answer: A. The scope of the unit.
The scope is the topic the teacher is teaching in his unit.

(Rigorous) (Skill 4.5.1)

46. **An excellent example of how cognition moves from elementary to more advanced is:**

    A. Vygotsky's ZPD

    B. Bloom's taxonomy

    C. Gardner's multiple intelligences

    D. Dewey's social theory

    Answer: B. Bloom's taxonomy.
    Bloom's taxonomy, which moves from elementary to more advanced skills, is an excellent example of how cognition develops over time.

(Rigorous) (Skill 4.5.1)

47. **A child who is developing jumping, running, and handwriting is working on her:**

    A. Affective domain

    B. Psychomotor domain

    C. Interpersonal domain

    D. None of the above

    Answer: B. Psychomotor domain.
    The psychomotor domain is focused on motor skills and how well a student can perform a sequence of kinesthetic skills.

(Average) (Skill 4.5.3)

48. **Observable behavior may include:**

    A. How much Timothy likes math

    B. How often Javier raised his hand during math

    C. How many times Javier answered correctly

    D. Both B and C

    Answer: D. Both B and C.
    Observable behavior is any behavior that is observable and quantifiable.

(Easy) (Skill 4.5.4)

49. **Which word would NOT be useful in writing a measurable objective?**

    A. Describe

    B. Evaluate

    C. Create

    D. Learn

    Answer: D. Learn.
    Learn is a subjective term and therefore not observable or quantifiable.

(Easy) (Skill 4.6.1)

50. **If a child is struggling in reading and has a low performance on many assessments, he needs:**

    A. Enrichment

    B. Remediation

    C. No interventions

    D. Peer tutoring

    Answer: B. Remediation.
    Remediation is used when a child has shown a consistent lack of understanding in a concept.

(Average) (Skill 4.7.3)

51. **A group of lessons centered on the geography of the Far East would be categorized as:**

    A. A thematic unit

    B. An interdisciplinary unit

    C. Using models

    D. Formative assessments

    Answer: A. A thematic unit.
    A thematic unit is a group of lessons organized around a particular theme, idea, or concept.

(Average) (Skill 4.7.5)

52. **What is the purpose of interdisciplinary instruction?**

    A. It gives students an in-depth understanding of a topic

    B. It provides real-life experience

    C. It gives students a well-rounded, view of a topic from multiple perspectives

    D. All of the above

    Answer: D. All of the above.
    All of the above are benefits of and reasons to pursue interdisciplinary instruction.

(Average) (Skill 4.7.6)

53. **Which is a challenge that interdisciplinary teachers may face?**

    A. Lack of teacher interest

    B. Lack of student interest

    C. Teacher protectiveness

    D. Difficulty of teamwork

    Answer: C. Teacher protectiveness.
    Often, teachers may feel protective of their subject matter and not want to share their lessons.

(Average) (Skill 4.7.7)

54. **A good use of a para educator's time is:**

    A. Making copies

    B. Managing student behavior

    C. Working with the most difficult students

    D. Managing a center

    Answer: D. Managing a center.
    Para educators can do some paperwork, but the most efficient use of their time is managing centers to keep students on task and engaged. Para educators are not special education teachers and are not trained to work with the most difficult students, so that may overwhelm them.

(Rigorous) (Skill 5.1)

55. **Louise always gets straight As. She does well on every assessment and is engaged in class. Her teacher wants to find out why this is happening. She looks at Louise's home life and her peer relationships and talks with her to find the answer. This type of analysis is called:**

    A. Inductive reasoning

    B. Deductive reasoning

    C. Questioning

    D. Critical thinking

    Answer: A. Inductive reasoning.
    Inductive reasoning moves from the specific information (peer and home life, interviews, etc.) to a generalization (why she is succeeding in class).

(Average) (Skill 5.1)

56. **The first thing a student should see when she walks into the classroom is:**

    A. The homework for that day

    B. The behavior incentive chart

    C. The goals and objectives for that day

    D. Seatwork

    Answer: C. The goals and objectives for that day.
    Goals and objectives should be posted clearly each day. Before a student starts any work, she should know why she is doing it. The next thing the student should see should be the bell work or seatwork for that day.

(Easy) (Skill 5.1)

57. **Basic recall is:**

A. A high level of comprehension

B. The ability to synthesize

C. An elementary understanding of concepts

D. The ability to evaluate

Answer: C. An elementary understanding of concepts.
Basic recall is the first level of Bloom's taxonomy, and it means that a student has the first level of understanding of a concept.

(Easy) (Skill 5.2.1)

58. **If a teacher stands in front of the class and shows a PowerPoint presentation on a topic, he is using which type of instruction?**

A. Direct instruction

B. Indirect instruction

C. Independent instruction

D. Experiential instruction

Answer: A. Direct instruction.
Direct instruction is the most traditional type of instruction. Often the teacher will walk around the room, giving students information through a PowerPoint presentation or just by speaking. Older students may take notes or fill out a worksheet.

(Average) (Skill 5.2.1)

59. **Homework is which type of instruction?**

A. Direct instruction

B. Indirect instruction

C. Independent instruction

D. Experiential instruction

Answer: C. Independent instruction.
Homework is a chance for independent practice, which is independent instruction.

(Average) (Skill 5.3.1)

60. **How long should an average lecture be for elementary students?**

A. 10–15 minutes

B. 15–20 minutes

C. 30 minutes

D. 45 minutes

Answer: A. 10–15 minutes.
Keep lectures for elementary students short to maintain their attention keep them engaged.

(Average) (Skill 5.3.2)

61. **Inquiry learning is most useful in which subject area?**

A. English

B. Science

C. Math

D. Social Studies

Answer: B. Science.
Because science is inquiry-based, inquiry learning is most useful in this subject area.

(Rigorous) (Skill 5.3.2)

62. The following is an example of which literacy strategy?

    "Joe loves books. In fact, Joe has many _____ at his house. Many of the books are about horses and farms. _____ are places where animals live."

    A. Reading for meaning

    B. Running records

    C. Cloze procedures

    D. None of the above

    Answer: C. Cloze procedures.
    A cloze procedure measures reading and comprehension ability. After the first sentence, a few words are missing. Students use prediction skills to find the missing words.

(Average) (Skill 5.3.4)

63. All of the following are examples of experiential learning EXCEPT:

    A. Field trips

    B. Direct instruction

    C. Role play

    D. Experiments

    Answer: B. Direct instruction.
    In direct instruction, students passively absorb information.

(Easy) (Skill 5.3.5)

64. Brainstorming should be done at what point in the writing process?

    A. At the beginning

    B. At the end

    C. In the middle of drafting

    D. Whenever the child needs it

Answer: A. At the beginning.
Before writing, a child should brainstorm. Brainstorming could be done with a peer or by using a graphic organizer.

(Rigorous) (Skill 5.4.1)

65. When a student associates multiplication with addition, she is showing which type of learning?

    A. Collaborative learning

    B. Problem solving

    C. Transfer learning

    D. Critical thinking

    Answer: C. Transfer learning.
    Transfer is when learning about one situation (addition) affects a student's learning about a new concept (multiplication). This student, who associated one concept with another, is experiencing positive transfer.

(Easy) (Skill 5.4.2)

66. When a student is comparing two stories, she should look for:

    A. Similarities

    B. Differences

    C. Both

    D. Neither

    Answer: A. Similarities.
    Comparing means similarities, so the student should look for things that are alike.

(Average) (Skill 5.4.2)

67. **When a small child sorts toys by color, she is showing which type of cognitive learning?**

    A. Predicting

    B. Categorizing

    C. Analyzing

    D. Contrasting

    Answer: B. Categorizing.
    When a child categorizes, she puts things into groups based on one characteristic.

(Rigorous) (Skill 5.4.2)

68. **When a teacher asks her students to perform a picture walk, she is asking them to use which skill?**

    A. Summarizing

    B. Decision making

    C. Sequencing

    D. Inferring

    Answer: D. Inferring.
    Inferring is taking clues from a piece of writing or a book and drawing conclusions about them.

(Average) (Skill 5.5.1)

69. **A young child who is told not to eat a cookie but then eats it as soon as the adult walks away does not have very strong skills in which area?**

    A. Scaffolding

    B. Modeling

    C. Self-regulation

    D. None of the above

Answer: C. Self-regulation.
Self-regulation skills are very difficult for young children. These skills develop later, when children can control their impulses and understand consequences.

(Average) (Skill 5.5.1)

70. **Mr. Cameron sets up three centers in his room, each of which practices rhyming. The first center asks students to play a matching game. The second asks students to write a poem, and the third is a teacher-run center where students jump on words that rhyme. Mr. Cameron is practicing which type of instruction?**

    A. Differentiated instruction

    B. Guided practice

    C. Scaffolding

    D. Coaching

Answer: A. Differentiated instruction.
Mr. Cameron is practicing differentiated instruction. In this practice, a teacher sets up various learning stations, all of which have the same goal but use different learning styles.

ANSWER TO CONSTRUCTED RESPONSE FOR TEST ONE:

A strong answer will include the following concepts, but is not limited to these concepts.

- Examine and discuss the various ethnicities in the class

- Examine and discuss the various academic levels in the class

- Examine and discuss the various socioeconomic challenges some of these students may face

- Discuss the varying personalities evident from the journal

Challenges could include language barriers, socioeconomic difficulties, motivation, hunger, and shelter (the first two levels of Maslow's hierarchy of needs).

In this section, the writer could talk about Gloria Ladson-Billings and the ideas behind culturally responsive classrooms. Outside literacies can be brought in to motivate students. By using challenges as tools, the teacher can create a behavior management system that connects peers and encourages collaborative learning.

Mrs. Dodd is having many management problems, but a few mentioned could have to do with the following:

- Leader personalities running the class in a negative way

- Students coming to class unprepared

- Students not understanding objectives

Solutions could include the following:

- Using leaders in a positive way by giving them jobs in the class

- Giving students a collaborative system in which they are responsible for one another's materials

- Placing posters on the outside of the door to encourage students to bring correct materials to class

- Creating new classroom rules with student help

The idea behind good examples should be to keep students engaged with authentic activities that are meaningful in their lives.

Jobs

for

Teachers

Find out more at

XAMonline.com

XAMonline.com

CPSIA information can be obtained
at www.ICGtesting.com
Printed in the USA
LVOW03s1600120716

496015LV00014B/465/P

9 781607 874461